F

A Pilgrim's Companion

by

David Baldwin

To Pope John Paul II who in life
dignified Life, and in his last
days dignified death.

*All booklets are published thanks to the
generous support of the members of the
Catholic Truth Society*

CATHOLIC TRUTH SOCIETY
PUBLISHERS TO THE HOLY SEE

CONTENTS

～ ROME - THE ETERNAL CITY ～

There is no other place in the world such as Rome that portrays the story of Christianity - and the human condition - on such an expansive and vivid, yet compact tapestry. It presents a wealth of physical evidence reaching back through the millennia, and in so doing, evokes many emotions, rekindles many memories, and brings to light fresh sentiments and perspectives about one's Christian faith, as seen through the places, people and events - past and present - that drove it forward, and continues to do so, in such a powerful and enduring manner.

And, of course, it is more than just a place. From it emanates, "The Church of Rome, expression of the whole Christian community and Mother of all Churches, and is projected towards the definitive city of God, place of eternal joy. In their journey towards her, all pilgrims are welcomed to a joyful pause in order to contemplate and experience awe for the beauty of being Christians. Or, in any case, to come in contact with the event of Christ, who, in the Church lives and moves towards every person 'from every nation, race, tribe and language' (*Rev* 7:9). 'What do we see that the disciples did not see? The Church spread among all peoples'. (St Augustine)".*

*From the Official Vatican Guide to the Jubilee Year 2000.

Touch with your own hands

Despite the modern convenience of plane, car or coach; despite all the trappings and manifestations of our own age evident in the city, the modern pilgrim can still indulge in that sense of ancient pilgrimage whilst exploring the wealth that Rome imparts - spiritual, cultural and physical. One can immerse oneself in the detail, or view a broad panorama, or both. In welcoming pilgrims to Rome for the Jubilee, Cardinal Etchegaray sums it up beautifully: "You will see a city like all others, yet unique in its mission. You will walk along streets marked by time and by man's hand, and yet the site of something that surpasses time, and goes beyond man. You will visit magnificent artistic monuments from the past, but they are still alive today, unlike the Greek temples or the Pyramids... you who believe in Christ, when you arrive in this city, you will be able almost to touch with your own hands the wonderful miracle of you being a Christian, of your belonging to the Church".

A pilgrim's companion

The purpose of this small book is fourfold: as a personal 'armchair pilgrimage' for those who wish, but for whatever reason, are unable to go; to inform, and maybe even give the final push for those who may have a hankering to go; for those planning to go - or are on their

way - to suggest some sort of structure on which to hang
their pilgrimage - particularly useful for the 'freelance
pilgrim', but also offering additional insight to those who
go on organised tour groups; and lastly, to rekindle the
memories of those who have been before, possibly re-
igniting a desire to re-visit this beguiling, extraordinary
and endlessly fascinating place.

This is not a guidebook in the conventional sense: the
market is awash with these. It is designed as a handy
'slip-in-the-pocket' companion to supplement the guide
book and provide a personal insight to your pilgrimage,
along with prayers and meditations to accompany you on
your way. It necessarily restricts itself to those holy
places and events in Rome; there are of course many
other sides to the city, which you also may want to
experience and enjoy, and those are adequately covered
in the more conventional guide books.

How to use this companion

The book is structured in distinct Sections, offering
'pilgrim strands' that you can either follow in entirety, or
pluck bits out of each, and weave your own plaits. I offer
a specific starting point to your journey, by going back to
the days of the early Church; then, in complete contrast,
there is a Section on Rome Today, giving an idea of the
weekly events in and around the Vatican that you may
wish to attend; then, a Section on St Peter's to help you

get to grips with this wonderful Basilica. There then follows three separate pilgrim strands: Our Lady in Rome, The Pilgrimage to the Seven Churches, and The Saints in Rome, from which you can 'pick and mix' as you wish. Lastly, a suggested ending point to your journey. As you will be visiting 'spaces-present' through the three millennia of 'times-past', there is a brief Timeline Section to help put things into some sort of historical context; and finally, to help with time and distance, and to save you too much poring over maps, I give groupings of venues that are within reasonable walking distance of each other.

A couple of tips

One tip that you may find useful. On entering many of the churches and buildings in Rome, one can be overwhelmed with the splendour and enormity of it all, and it bothered me, that in not being able to take it all in, I would miss out on important detail. But at that rate I could have been in danger of not even moving on from the entrance portico, let alone progressing through the church or my pilgrimage! I started suffering from information overload and an overdose of prior homework in my efforts to sort out exactly where I was and what I was going to see. To overcome this I soon learned to accept, firstly, that overall impression was the best I should settle for if I was not going to be totally bogged down, and secondly, to be highly selective if I wanted to concentrate fully on something that caught my eye or imagination.

The transport system in Rome is plentiful and cheap, so it is well worth getting to grips with the not-too-difficult Metro, tram and bus system. In planning your day, you must take into account the delightful Italian custom of the afternoon siesta - many shops and establishments, including churches - close between one-ish and three-ish, sometimes longer, but to compensate, they are open later in the evening; don't make a special journey to visit somewhere over these hours without first checking opening times, most major guide books indicate these.

Seek as a Pilgrim

Finally, today's ethos and pace of life is full of target setting, ticking boxes, high achieving and high speed. Un-clutch from all this at a very early stage: your pilgrimage should not be seen as some sort of endurance test or marathon! You have come to the place to meet, marvel and ponder over those who have gone before us, many giving their lives for the Faith; you have come to share and celebrate this treasure with your many thousands of fellow pilgrims, who have come from all corners of the earth, proclaiming the Universal Church; you have come to seek reassurance and continuity, through the presence of the Holy Father, Christ's Chief Vicar on earth, the direct successor to Peter. You have come to seek a deeper understanding of yourself and your Christian faith. Above all, you have come to seek Jesus, Our Lord. Savour it sweetly and slowly. The Peace of the Lord be with you! Welcome to the Eternal City!

> *I lift up my eyes to you*
> *who are enthroned in heaven.*
> (*Ps* 123:1)

❧ THE BEGINNING ❧

Arrival

Unless you are with an organised tour, where your itinerary will more than likely be pre-set, there is always the problem for the 'freelancer' as to where to start, and how to sensibly progress on the wonderful task of your pilgrim journey through Rome. I would imagine the innate desire of any pilgrim arriving in Rome is to head straight for the magnificent Basilica of St Peter. It was certainly mine, and I did. It seemed to be the one sure place to start, and for one thing, even as a complete stranger in Rome, it is not difficult to find! And having achieved this, it does make you feel that you have 'arrived', it gives you confidence, and provides an anchor point for the rest of your stay. I was not entirely disappointed with this premise, but a lot more of St Peter's later. Having got this initial first-impression, 'courtesy call' to St Peter's under my belt, my own feeling was to go right back to the beginning in time of the early Church in Rome, and to try and get a sense of what those first days were all about.

Prayer

Come, Father of light,	Send a spark of your fire
Come, God of Love,	Within my soul
Form my prayer within me,	To enflame it
Show me the truth,	And fill it with God.

Come, Holy Spirit,
maker of Martyrs
and confessors,
Apostles and prophets,
Great heroes
and great hearts.
Your guidance alone
did my Saviour follow;
So that I may imitate Him,
Guide me likewise.

(Saint Louis-Marie Grignion de Montfort)

The early Christians

There is little hard, historical evidence as to the exact
circumstances and identities of those first Christians
who came to Rome immediately after the Resurrection
and in the ensuing early years. No doubt they were
traders, travellers, migrants, even returning officials and
their households, all, who directly or indirectly, had
come under the extraordinary influence of the Christ
and His followers in the remote Roman colony of Judea.
That there was a Christian community to be reckoned
with is in no doubt, as in AD 57/58 Paul wrote his letter
to the Romans. All that can be gleaned from the letter
are the occasional allusions that it was a mixed
community of Jewish and non-Jewish converts who may
have looked down on one another. Paul's promise,
"Then I shall come to you, if God wills, for a happy
time of relaxation in your company" (*Rom* 15:32) was
fulfilled in AD 61, although not quite in the relaxing
circumstances that he envisaged!

The Church Domine Quo Vadis? on the Appian Way.

Similarly, Peter's residence and death in Rome is beyond contention, although exact dates are obscure. There is some evidence that he came to Rome as early as AD 42, and over the next twenty five years led the nascent church as the first Vicar of Christ, appointed by Christ himself, "You are Peter and on this rock I will build my community.... I will give you the keys of the kingdom of heaven..." (*Mt* 16:18,19). According to Origen, Peter was 'crucified at Rome with his head downwards, as he himself had desired to suffer'.

Persecution

Up to this period the fledgling Christian community was largely left alone by the Roman authorities, but in AD 64, a fire, said to have been started by the Emperor Nero, devastated Rome. Nero sought the scapegoats from the Christian community through large scale persecution, graphically described by a historian of the time, Tacitus, "Besides being put to death they were made to serve as objects of amusement. They were clad in hides of beasts and torn to death by dogs; others were crucified, others set on fire to serve to illuminate when daylight failed". According to tradition, Paul was also martyred during this persecution, by being beheaded, some say on the same day (29th June) and year as Peter, near Rome at the Aquae Salviae (now Tre Fontane) in AD 67.

Whilst not as widespread and persistent as may be popularly made out, persecution did continue intermittently against the Christians in Rome under other Emperors - Domitian (81-96), Marcus Aurelius (161-180), Decius (249-251) and Valerian (253). Low level discrimination however, also pervaded throughout this period. The common citizen, in the words of the historian, Hibbert, "was suspicious of their exclusiveness, their rites and their supposed 'abominations' which included cannibalism - regarding them as alien trouble makers and revolutionaries, a danger to the state and a blasphemy against the ancient gods of Rome".

But despite persecution at whatever level, the faithful would not be suppressed, and where martyrs went to their death, others came forward to take their place. St Perpetua, married, aged 22 with babe in arms, describes her trial in 203, and the desperate pleading of her father to renounce her faith; this she refused to do, "Then the judge passed sentence on us all and condemned us to the wild beasts. In great joy we returned to our prison". It is estimated that in Diocletian's reign (284) there were about thirty thousand Christians in Rome, coming together in groups to worship, usually in private houses known as *tituli*, and, since St Peter's time, had been shepherded by thirty three bishops, or popes. As with many periods of persecution, throughout the world, throughout time, the Emperors' brutish attempts at eradication only served to strengthen the Church.

DOMINE QUO VADIS?

The journey begins

Against this background my specific starting point was the small, humble church of Domine, Quo Vadis? just outside the city walls beyond St Sebastian's Gate, on the Appian Way. It does not figure prominently in the guide books (another reason for going!), and whilst the church itself is not early Christian, it depicts a marvellously emotional and symbolic start, not only to the Church's journey, but for your own journey as well. It commemorates the occasion, as legend tells it, where St Peter, the first Pope, was on the Old Appian Way, leaving Rome, having been persuaded by his fellow Christians to flee for his safety, and sees a vision of the Lord. To truly relive the feeling of this event it may even be fitting to follow St Peter's short, putative journey away from Rome, by walking the short distance from St Sebastian's Gate, along the Appian Way to this small church.

Whilst the historicity of this event is not entirely certain there have been many written accounts of it dating back to earliest times, stemming from the apocryphal Acts of the Apostle Peter, to Acts of Pseudus Linus in the fourth century: "Thus Peter, on hearing these pleas and being of a sensitive nature - was won over by these laments, and replied: 'None of you will accompany me. I

shall change my clothes and I shall go alone.' The
following night, following the liturgical prayer, he said
goodbye to his friends, entrusting them to God with his
blessing, and he left alone. He was about to walk through
the city gates when he saw Christ coming towards him.
He paid reverence to Him and said, 'Lord, where are you
going?' ('*Domine, quo vadis?*'). Christ replied, 'I am
going to Rome to be crucified again.' Peter replied,
'Lord, I am going back to follow you.' Then the Lord
rose up towards the heavens. Peter watched Him go and
wept with joy. When he came to himself, he understood
the words referred to his own martyrdom, namely, how
the Lord would suffer in him, as He suffers in all those
who are chosen. Thus, Peter returned to the city joyously,
glorifying God. He told his friends that the Lord had
come to meet him and told him he would be crucified
again in him." (Account taken from the church booklet).

Domine Quo Vadis?

This lovely, rather careworn little church would also be
one of my 'havens of peace', away from the, at times,
overwhelming splendour of the Rome churches and the
bustle and hubbub of the city. Being dedicated to Our
Lady, it has above the tabernacle a fourteenth century
fresco showing a serene Madonna and Child. A small
side altar to the Sacred Heart has above it a fresco of St
Francis. In the centre of the small aisle is a copy of a

pair of footprints, said to be Christ's, imprinted in the
stone on which he was standing during his encounter
with St Peter. To one side, an image of the Divine
Mercy, and a statue of St Therese of Liseux. It is
perfect. By the entrance is a bust of Henryk
Sienkiewicz, the Polish author and Nobel prize winner
(1905) who wrote the book *Quo Vadis*. Here is the ideal
place to take a good pause and to recollect oneself
before setting off, asking: '*Quo vadis?*': where have I
got to, where am I going?

Meditation

*Go with us on the paths by which we make our
pilgrimage to you and find our true selves in you. May
there emerge in each one of us the man of faith, hope
and charity, courageous in self-discipline and pure in
heart, joyful in confidence, and persevering in patience.
We are still only at the beginning of all these paths, for
the goal is in your infinite distance. Yet we are already
and always at our end, for you, our goal, live in us in
your Holy Spirit. All is contained in you: beginning and
end, battle and victory, our weakness and your strength
- and you are ours. And we and you, Lord Jesus Christ,
are the Father's, to whom through you in the Holy Spirit
be all glory for ever and ever.*

(Father Hugo Rahner SJ)

Prayer

My Lord God, I have no idea where I am going.
I do not see the road ahead of me.
I cannot know for certain where it will end.
Nor do I really know myself,
and the fact that I think I am following your will
does not mean that I am actually doing so.
But I believe that my desire to please you
does in fact please you.
And I hope that I have that desire in all that I am doing.
I hope that I will never do anything
apart from that desire.
And I know that if I do this you will lead me
by the right road, though I may know nothing about it.
Therefore will I trust you always,
though I may seem to be lost
and in the shadow of death.
I will not fear, for you are ever with me,
and you will never leave me to face my perils alone.

(Thomas Merton, A Prayer)

Whilst the stuff of legend is always open to question - and the more cynical one is, the bigger the questions - it is a legend that certainly found favour with Pope John Paul II. On his visit to Domine Quo Vadis? in 1982, amongst other favourable comments, he said, "It is a legend, but a legend that has found a deep appeal and a special credibility in the hearts of Christians... it is a place which has a special importance in the history of Rome and in the history of the Church."

Having spent some time of reflective prayer and meditation in this quiet haven, my thoughts then turned from St Peter, the first shepherd of the Church, to his flock. And for evidence of this, my journey now took me a short walking distance from Domine Quo Vadis? up the Old Appian Way, to the catacombs - that vast network of underground burial chambers constructed over the first three centuries to inter the Christian dead in safety and with dignity, and described contemporaneously as 'the cradle of Christianity and the Archives of the primitive Church'. There are a number of catacomb sites along the Appian Way - Saint Sebastian, Domitilla, and Saint Callistus.

THE CATACOMBS

Following earlier Jewish tradition and Roman law at the time, but also in response to the periods of persecution, the early Christian community interred their dead underground, and outside the city limits, to minimise interference from the authorities and hostile pagans. Thus developed the catacombs on the outskirts of Rome, an ever expanding warren of large underground tunnels with numerous side niches for the interments, and sometimes down to five levels, dug out of the soft tufa rock, to become the resting place of thousands - from prominent saint, pope or heroic martyr, to obscure citizen. The larger ones were dug in the grounds of the better-off fellow Christians, where, during persecution, worship meetings were also sometimes held in secret, out of sight of the authorities. Between the late first century and early fourth century some seventy underground cemetery systems had been developed, ranging from the very extensive, with nearly a hundred thousand graves, to the lesser, with only a few hundred.

With the freedom given to Christianity by the Emperor Constantine in the fourth century there was no longer any requirement to go underground. Many of the catacombs now became places of pilgrimage to venerate the illustrious buried there. Later in the fifth century extensive plundering of the catacombs by invaders prompted later popes to transfer the remains of the martyrs to the protection of the many churches in Rome, within the city's walls. The catacombs thus fell into disuse and disrepair, even their exact whereabouts being largely forgotten. It was not until the sixteenth century that they were rediscovered, often by accident, and eventually many were opened up again as pilgrim venues.

Catacombs of Saint Callistus

The site of the catacombs named after their first custodian, Saint (Pope) Callistus I (217-222), was my particular preference. These catacombs, believed to be the oldest formal burial ground in Rome, are currently in the custody of the Salesians of Don Bosco, and lie within extensive, tranquil and green-swarded grounds, with pine-lined approaches to the catacomb site. It is when walking along these peaceful approach paths that you can start to gather your thoughts about those early Christians, many who suffered persecution and violent death, but many others, in peaceful times, lived out their lives and died peacefully in their Christian faith.

Living signs of the early Church

From the small group of warm, rustic brick buildings, nestling amongst neatly kept hedges and palm trees at ground level, there is nothing to indicate the vast warren of about twelve miles of underground galleries, going down to four levels, and where nearly half a million people were buried, that lie below. Tour groups are sorted by language, and after a preliminary briefing, led below. As soon as one enters the cool, damp, silent tunnels one feels a sense of wonderment at the sheer complexity of this underground construction, and also, examining the niches cut at various levels in the tunnel walls where the bodies were laid to rest, a feeling of peace and serenity. One notices immediately how short the niches, or *loculi*, are, for the people of those times were shorter of stature; one notices with some poignancy the tiny ones for infants and children, the small indentations carved for oil lamps to light the way, the many symbols and messages, some personal, some symbolic of the faith, carved in the walls. As you gaze in wonder, and in prayer, upon these ancient scratchings you somehow find yourself connecting with not only the person who carved them but also for whom they were intended.

On the tour route underground one also comes across much larger chambers carved into the rock: the Crypt of the Popes, sometimes called 'the little Vatican', as nine popes are buried here, along with other dignitaries of the third century Church; the Cubicles of the Sacraments, consisting of five family tombs, but significant for their frescoes depicting sacramental life of the early Church - Baptism and the Eucharist; and that of St Cecilia, an early third century martyr.

St Cecilia

St Cecilia's Crypt is particularly moving, because there, lying in the place she was interred is the copy of a statue (1599), carved just as her body was found, incorrupt, laid out full length on her side, her head turned away, but with the cut mark of the sword clearly depicted on her throat, and with three fingers open on the right hand and one on the left - a last gesture of defiance to her executioners and a statement of her great faith - the Trinity, and the Unity of God. St Cecilia's life and martyrdom in the third

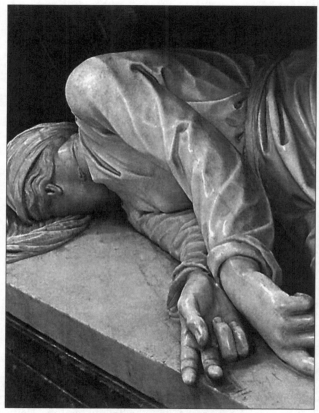

Statue of St Cecilia, Church of St Cecilia in Trastevere and Catacombs of St Callistus.

century is brought to us by tradition, emanating from fifth
century documentation. In her Passion, her execution was
reportedly botched, and she took three days to die, praying
and preaching all the while. Today, she is the patron saint
of singers, poets and musicians. Any one wishing to
follow St Cecilia in more detail can do so by going to the
church dedicated to her: St Cecilia in Trastevere, another
of the few oases of peace in amongst the bustle of Rome.

Spirituality of the Catacombs

An early believer likened the catacombs to the holy
Jerusalem, a city ennobled with the blood of the martyrs,
when he carved on the plastered wall near the Crypt of
the Popes his thoughts, which can still be read today,
"*Gerusale, civitas et ornamentum martyrum Dei...*"
("Jerusalem, city and ornament of God's martyrs"). In
picking up on these thoughts, and by contemplating what
the catacombs represent, either during one's visit, or
subsequently, one can dwell on many strands of
spirituality that they evoke: Christocentric, Sacramental,
Eschatological, Biblical, or the spirituality of Silence,
listening to what Gregory the Great once referred to as
the 'uproar of silence'. Whilst quietly threading one's
way through the catacombs, listening to and wondering at
the guide's explanation of various aspects, one realises
that down here words are not necessary: the eloquence of
silence says it all. In the words of Pope John Paul II, "In

the silence of the catacombs, the pilgrim can rediscover or revive his religious identity on a sort of spiritual journey that, by starting from the first testimonies of the faith, brings him to the reasons for the new evangelisation and to its demands."

There is a lovely passage in Sienkiewicz's book *Quo Vadis* describing the Christian worship that took place in the catacomb areas in Nero's time, as witnessed by the fictitious Vinicius, a Roman nobleman, "But suddenly a few pine torches flamed beside the entrance to the catacombs...the light became sharper. A strange hushed chant started quietly among the waiting thousands, and it gradually grew louder. Vinicius never heard this kind of music before. He picked up the same deep note of longing and regret he had heard on the road, hummed and sung in low voices by occasional passers-by earlier in the night, but now, multiplied by a thousand voices, it swelled into a vast imploring sigh. Faith and a profound sense of hope and suffering rang in this pleading chorus, becoming clearer and stronger and more pronounced and pressing, until it seemed that the entire burial ground, along with the sandpits, hillocks and open lands around it was singing to the stars along with the people".

A little way further up the Appian Way are the catacombs (and Basilica) of St Sebastian, (details of which are given below, at p. 77, Pilgrimage to the Seven Churches.)

Meditation

I urge you, then, brothers, remembering the mercies of God to offer your bodies as a living sacrifice, dedicated and acceptable to God, that is the kind of worship for you, as sensible people. Do not model your behaviour on the contemporary world, but let the renewing of your minds transform you, so that you may discern for yourselves what is the will of God - what is good and acceptable and mature. (Rom 12:1-2)

Prayer

O God, you enriched the first fruits of the Church in Rome with the blood of the martyrs. Through the shining example of so many courageous witnesses strengthen us in faith, so that we can joyfully gather the fruits of their sacrifice.

THREE SPECIAL PLACES

The Colosseum

This gigantic amphitheatre was built by the Emperors of the Flavian dynasty between AD 72 and AD 80 for the purpose of entertaining Roman citizens on a grand scale with gladiatorial combat to full scale naval battles when the arena was specially flooded for this purpose. Its distinct elliptical shape, 617 feet long, with its columns, arches and ever rising tiers of terraces reaching to over

160 feet, was capable of seating 70,000 spectators. A huge awning would be hoisted over the top to shield spectators from the sun. However, contrary to popular belief, there is no hard evidence that this arena was ever used for the martyrdom of Christians - this was carried out in the nearby Roman Circus.

By the sixth century these great spectacles came to a close, and this magnificent edifice fell into gradual abandonment and dismantlement - its main purpose being a 'quarry' to provide stonework for many major building projects in Rome, St Peter's and St John Lateran included. This thankfully came to a halt in the 18th century when Benedict XIV declared it 'holy ground' as a memorial to Christian martyrs, and forbade further desecration. He installed the Stations of the Cross in the arena, and to this day the Pope follows Christ's Passion ending at the Colosseum on Good Friday. Although the original Stations no longer exist, a large, lone, plain Cross stands for all to see at ground level on the north east side. The Colosseum is one of the world's enduring icons - as immediately identifiable as Big Ben or the Statue of Liberty. It is a huge tourist attraction, and restoration is ongoing to preserve and enhance it, for apart from the revenue it attracts, the Roman authorities may also be mindful of St Bede's prophecy in the 8th century, "As long as the Colosseum remains standing, so will Rome; when the Colosseum falls... so will Rome...and when Rome falls, the world will fall too".

The Pantheon

The Pantheon is a remarkable church in many ways - it is circular, has no windows, claims the biggest brick-built dome in the world - atop which is a large round aperture completely open to the elements, and unlike the many present-day Roman buildings of its time, its architecture is perfectly preserved from the days it was built. This was a pagan temple built by the Emperor Hadrian in about 118-125, dedicated to all the gods (hence 'Pantheon'). It was consecrated as a church in 609 by Pope Boniface IV, being dedicated to St Maria ad Martyres. It is fronted by an immense, pillared portico, and you enter the church through the imposing, original bronze doors, still said to be swinging on their original hinges! Once inside, your eyes take in the unadorned but superb, soaring, coffered dome, and then up to the *oculus* - the twenty seven foot wide circular aperture at its crown. From it you can you can trace the circle of bright sunlight as it creeps round the inside of the dome; when it rains, the water is caught in cleverly concealed drains in the floor to prevent puddling. The dome is 142 feet in diameter - slightly larger than St Peter's - and as the height from floor to top is also 142 feet, the whole forms a perfectly symmetrical sphere sitting within the 'cylinder' of the church. Here lies the tombs of the modern Kings of Italy, and that of the artist, Raphael.

Mamertine Prison

If you are in the area of the Gesu, or visiting its adjacent rooms of St Ignatius of Loyola (see p. 94, Saints in Rome), or sightseeing round the Victor Emmanuel Monument (*Il Vittoriano*), it will be well worthwhile visiting the nearby Mamertine Prison. Don't expect anything spectacular or on a large scale, but in the small, dank, cramped underground cells you might just get a bit of a shiver when you reflect on this being the place where Ss Peter and Paul, and many others, were incarcerated before their execution. On the lower level, the *tullianum*, are several interesting items to ponder: the spring, which legend has it miraculously appeared for St Peter to baptise his jailers; a small altar, above which is a bronze bas relief depicting this event, and, with a lovely small detail on the altar-front of the upside-down cross in which manner Peter was crucified; the marble column to which it is said Peter and Paul were chained. The stairway down to this area is of a later time, the usual method of entrance was being flung down the opening clearly apparent on the ceiling above!

On the next level up, in the slightly larger, but no less dank cell, is the Mamertine prison, quite bare apart from an 18th century altar, above which are wooden busts of Ss Peter and Paul. The two chambers together are known as St Pietro in Carcere. From here you emerge up some steps back into daylight with relief! The church above the prison is the 16th century St Joseph of the Carpenters, underneath which, between church floor and prison ceiling, is the Chapel of the Crucifix, where a 16th century crucifix is venerated. In effect, when looking at a simple cross section of this complex, there are altars and churches, all above one another, at four different levels.

Wherever your starting point may be, I would now like to describe, in the next Section, some of those live events and opportunities that take place in Rome over the week, to help you plan your other visits round them, if you so wish.

❧ ROME TODAY ❧

WEEKLY EVENTS

Holy Father's Audience

Whilst following your pilgrimage through times-past in spaces-present, one can also take part in events-present in spaces-past. And surely one of the great and enduring Catholic gatherings must be the Holy Father's weekly General Audience, usually held every Wednesday morning in St Peter's Square during the warm weather season (indoors in the Paul VI Papal Audience Chamber during the winter months). It is here, that thousands gather, and patiently wait for the Pope's arrival. Every nationality under the sun must be present, in small or large groups, or as individuals. A front seat, secured early, at one of the transverse enclosure barriers, is a must, because the Holy Father is driven through the enclosures as he enters St Peter's Square.

His entry is greeted with huge enthusiasm and love, the clapping and cheering rippling along with his slow progress as he is driven through the enclosures. Then rather dramatically the vehicle turns and slowly mounts the wide, shallow steps leading up to the Basilica, and the Holy Father takes his place under the large red canopy set against the majestic backdrop of St Peter's, alongside his cardinals and priests. Down in front of him he surveys the thousands of people that look to him as the Vicar of Christ, the *Pontifex Maximus*, the Chief Shepherd. To one side, close to the podium, are selected visiting groups: religious, children, disabled, newly married brides and grooms glowing in their wedding finery. Some of these fortunate few will meet the Pope individually, but for the rest of us, we can only sit back, and collectively take part and rejoice in this great gathering of international prayer and love.

The Audience usually takes the form of a topical reflection given by the Pope, which, along with greetings read out in various languages from the cardinals on the podium; the Pope will also add his own greetings in the many languages of that day. One cannot help but be uplifted by the huge enthusiasm shown by those present: large groups cheering or whooping loudly when they are mentioned, acknowledged by a cheery wave from the Holy Father, to the respectful silence when the reflection or prayers are said. It is just about the right mixture of carnival and reverence, of outpouring joy and inward reflection. For me the most moving moment was being blessed by the Holy Father at the end, standing alongside those many thousands of my fellow Catholics in unity of prayer and communion with the Holy Father, but really having that strong feeling that the blessing was just for me.

Prayer - Special Intention for the Pope
Let us pray for our Holy Father, that the Lord who has chosen Him, grant him life and health and preserve him in his Holy Church. Father of Providence, look with love on our Shepherd on earth, your appointed successor to Saint Peter on whom you built your Church. May he be the visible centre and foundation of our unity in faith and love. Grant this through our Lord, Jesus Christ, your Son, who lives and reigns with you and the Holy Spirit, one God for ever and ever.

Sunday International Mass

Another fixed event worth attending is the International Mass celebrated in St Peter's on Sunday morning. Again, early arrival will secure a seat. It is an event which presents the Universal Church in all its universality, its majesty and its glory. When I attended there were sixteen cardinals and bishops, twenty six priests and two deacons concelebrating, and people from all over the world in the packed congregation. The Mass was sung Latin, and what with the magnificent choral and organ music, the heady smell of incense, the sun radiating through the amber rays surrounding the Holy Spirit in the stained glass window above the Altar of the Chair, the colour, the pomp, the ceremony, the great sense of occasion and solemnity, all only served to highlight and glorify this great mystery of the Eucharist, being celebrated again, as it was in those early, muted days in the catacombs and house churches in Rome, and indeed today, every minute of every day, somewhere round the world.

Sunday Angelus and Blessing

The last fixed, weekly event at which I would strongly recommend attendance is the Holy Father's Sunday blessing and Angelus for those who gather in St Peter's Square just before midday. In many ways it could be quite a prosaic and homely affair if it was not on such a grand scale, because far up on the top right hand corner of one of the tall buildings overlooking the square is an open window with the drapes, and a banner hanging from it, billowing in the breeze. Through this window one can just make out the figure of the Holy Father, but what one may lose in sight is certainly made up in sound by the superb amplification system in the Square. Again it is uplifting to be carried along by the enthusiasm and joy of the thousands there, heads upturned, waving banners, national and organisation flags, all clapping and cheering. The highlight of this particular event was, when praying the Angelus, thinking, wow! I am actually saying this with the Pope!

Prayer - the Angelus

The angel of the Lord declared unto Mary.
And she conceived by the Holy Spirit. Hail Mary...

Behold the handmaid of the Lord.
Be it done unto me according to Thy word. Hail Mary...

And the Word was made flesh.
And dwelt amongst us. Hail Mary...

Pray for us O Holy Mother of God.
That we may be made worthy of the promises of Christ.

Let us pray: Pour forth we beseech Thee O Lord,
Thy grace into our hearts, that we to whom the
Incarnation of Christ Thy Son was made known
by the message of an angel, may by His Passion
and Cross be brought to the glory of His Resurrection,
through the same Christ Our Lord. Amen.

Mass and Eucharistic Adoration

In contrast to the great occasion of the International Mass
in St Peter's were the other more modest but continuous
threads of Eucharistic participation running through my
Rome pilgrimage. Firstly, daily (evening) attendance of
Mass in a local parish church (Santa Maria delle Grazie)
not far from my hotel. It was a modern, large, unadorned
church, more functional than elegant, but a lovely place
to worship with the parishioners, and with as far as I

could see, no other tourists. Church and Mass devotion is obviously still strong in Rome, with healthy congregations, and one of the moments that moved me here was listening to the worshippers singing the Sanctus, the women singing strongly and with conviction in a raw, untutored manner, but with evocation and poignancy. This was the 'ordinary, every day' Church at worship, such a contrast and far cry from the splendour and pomp of St Peter's only two miles down the road! For those staying close to the Vatican City, I can also recommend the small, lovely church of St Anna for early evening Mass with local people. This church is just inside the Vatican City through the gate on Via di Porta Angelica, offering one of those rare occasions that you can enter this part of the City without official invitation!

Prayer

Come then,
good Shepherd,
bread divine,
Still show to us
thy mercy sign;
Oh, feed us,
still keep us thine;
So we may see
thy glories shine
in fields of immortality.

O thou, the wisest,
mightiest, best,
Our present food,
our future rest,
Come, make us each
thy chosen guest,
Co-heirs of thine,
and comrades blest
With saints whose
dwelling is with thee.

(St Thomas Aquinas)

Other places of Adoration

There were also other occasions to take advantage of
Eucharistic Adoration, of which Pope John Paul II was so
keen to promote. The major basilicas and larger churches all
have periods of Adoration in an appropriate side chapel,
including the Blessed Sacrament chapel in St Peter's, where,
despite the continual hum of people in the main basilica,
there reigned peace and quiet, a tangible sense of prayer and
reflection being conducted by the faithful from around the
world, all in the common purpose of kneeling before and
Adoring Our Lord. The church of St Bridget's also offers
periods of Adoration (see p. 90, Saints in Rome), and there
are no doubt other havens of Adoration that you may come
across, or be led to. Also in this category, if you happen to
be in the vicinity of the Victor Emmanuel Monument (*Il
Vittoriano*), there is a sublime, small, modern side chapel,
Capella la Madonnella de St Marco, directly off the
pavement of Piazza Venezia, that offers Adoration during
specified hours of the day. It is part of, but separate to, the
adjacent Basilica of St Marco.

Meditation
It is pleasant to spend time with him, to lie close to his
breast like the Beloved Disciple (cf Jn 13:25) and to feel
the infinite love present in his heart. If in our time
Christians must be distinguished above all by the 'art of
prayer', how can we not feel a renewed need to spend

time in spiritual converse, in silent adoration, in heartfelt
love before Christ present in the Most Holy Sacrament?
How often, dear brothers and sisters, have I experienced
this, and drawn from it strength, consolation and support?
(Pope John Paul II, Ecclesia de Eucharistica para 25).

THE VATICAN

Vatican City and Museums

It is an intriguing thought, that from the village-sized - in
terms of population (about 1000) and area (108 acres) - the
Vatican City dispenses major affairs of international state
and the spiritual care of over a billion people round the
world. Despite its diminutive size, it is an independent
sovereign state represented throughout the world. It has its
own army, currency, postal system and stamps, flag,
anthem, and the Head of State is the Pope. There is no
crime, poverty, unemployment or taxes! Along with various
administrative offices, and the large, private gardens, there
is a radio station and newspaper (*L'Osservatore Romano*).
Entrance is limited by invitation only, usually for those on
business directly linked to Vatican affairs.

The Vatican museums occupy a large area of the
Vatican City. They house the world's greatest collection
of Classical and Renaissance art. In terms of size and
scope they are, in a word - overwhelming! If you are a
'museum person' you may be in danger of not seeing

anything else of Rome! My purpose was in seeking a more reflective pilgrim spirituality, and the Museums were for me a short, 'overview' visit to gain impressions.

The Sistine Chapel

The Sistine Chapel of course must be seen, but one must exercise a level of detachment from the surrounding throng if one is to appreciate in any detail the staggering works of art depicted on the walls and ceiling. It is the official private chapel to the Pope, and is dedicated to Our Lady Assumed into Heaven. The wall paintings are by some of the finest artists of the time, although famously, it was Michelangelo who painted the magnificent ceiling fresco. This was commissioned by Pope Julius II, whose relationship with Michelangelo is described as 'fractious,' and much against his artistic instinct Michelangelo protested, "the place is wrong and no painter I"; he nonetheless undertook the work for over four years of exhausting and painstaking effort between 1508 and 1512. After the inaugural Mass in 1512, those who saw the result were such 'as to make everyone speechless with astonishment'.

This having left Michelangelo exhausted and ill, it is amazing that twenty four years later, and with his ongoing involvement with the building of St Peter's, he accepted Paul III's commission, and spent five years working alone, painting, what has been described as 'disturbing', the enormous Last Judgement fresco on the back wall of the Chapel. It is in this splendid setting, in what has been rather irreverently described as 'the world's most extraordinary polling station', that the College of Cardinals sit in conclave to elect a new Pope.

The Vatican Guard

Just to the left of the entrance doors to St Peter's Basilica is one of the few gates into the Vatican City. Guarding this gate, in their splendidly colourful and anachronistic uniforms of bright Medici blue, red and yellow, and largely unchanged since the Middle Ages, with their long, medieval halberds, are members of the Pontifical Swiss Guard, a force drawn exclusively from Swiss Catholics, who since 1506 have sworn allegiance to, and died in defence of the Pope. Their greatest sacrifice in executing this role came in 1527, during the sack of Rome, when 147 lost their lives. As a former military person I was impressed with their steadiness and bearing; they all looked young, fit, confident and professional military men.

Before you pick up on any of the pilgrim strands on offer in the ensuing sections, with the many events described above having taken place in and around St Peter's, it might be worth now, having a good look at this magnificent Basilica.

There is no permanent city for us here;
we are looking for the one that is yet to be. (*Heb* 13:14)

❦ St Peter's Basilica ❧

Some History

The Old St Peter's

Around the year AD 80, some thirteen years after Peter the Apostle, the first Pope and Bishop of Rome, was interred on Vatican Hill, a small oratory was built over the tomb by the third Pope, Cletus. This humble place of interment soon became the venue for devotion and veneration by pilgrims from all over the Roman Empire, coming to pay tribute to this fisherman of Galilee to whom Jesus entrusted His Church on earth. Just over two centuries later, in recognition of this holy site, the Emperor Constantine commissioned the building of a large, five-aisled basilica almost three hundred feet long and a hundred foot wide. It was consecrated in 326 by Pope St Silvester I and completed by 349 by Constantius, Constantine's son. It remained the centre of pilgrimage throughout those early centuries, also witnessing many splendid occasions, one of which was the Coronation of Charlemagne as the first Holy Roman Emperor on Christmas Day 800.

It also survived, by the respect and veneration it drew, even by invaders, the many sackings inflicted upon the city in those times. However, during the Saracen invasion of 846 even this esteem was violated, and the basilica was plundered. Attempts were made over the next centuries to make good the damage, but when the papacy withdrew, during the period of the so-called 'Babylonian captivity', to Avignon in the fourteenth century, the basilica fell into disrepair and neglect. The state of the Basilica, and indeed Rome at that time, prompted the commentator Petrarch to lament in the Holy Year of 1350, "The Lateran lies on the ground, and the Mother of all churches stands without a roof....the holy dwellings of St Peter and St Paul totter, and what was until recently the temple of the Apostles is a shapeless heap of ruins to excite pity in hearts of stone".

St Peter's rebuilt

When the papacy was finally restored to Rome by Gregory XI in 1376, further, rather piecemeal attempts, were made over the next hundred years or so to restore it to its former glory, but the accrued damage of the centuries was on such a scale as to prove futile. The planning for a replacement basilica started under Pope Nicholas V in 1452, but it was not until 1506 that the first stone of the new St Peter's was laid by Pope Julius II. The basilica was under construction for over a hundred years under the initial direction of the architect Donato Bramante. Many others succeeded him over the ensuing

years, but notably Michelangelo, who took on this huge
project aged 72 in 1547, continuing until his death some
sixteen years later. From the small human scale of the
exquisitely carved statue of the Pieta, to the mighty,
soaring construction of the dome, his hand and influence
prevails over much of the detail.

St Peter's is the largest church in the world, standing at
over six hundred feet long and four hundred and fifty feet
wide at the transepts, covering a staggering floor area of
six acres, and capable of holding eighty thousand people;
from ground level to the top of the cross on the dome is
four hundred and sixty feet. It contains 44 altars, 395
statues, 778 columns, and 99 oil lamps burn day and
night round the tomb of the Apostle. Much of the interior
decoration is Bernini's, of which his most prominent
work is the huge *baldacchino*, the magnificent canopy
above the papal altar, over ten stories high, supported by
four ornate twisted bronze pillars. The Basilica was
consecrated in 1626 by Urban VIII.

Enhancing and complementing the majesty of the
Basilica is St Peter's Square, the large piazza in front of
the church. In the centre of the piazza is the Egyptian
obelisk brought back as a trophy by the Emperor Caligula
to grace the Circus of Nero, the area over which the
Basilica and Square now stand. The obelisk reaches over
one hundred and fifty feet into the sky, and the hollow
cross on top of it is said to contain a fragment of the True

Cross. Reaching out from St Peter's, like two strong, welcoming arms, are the beautifully symmetrical and graceful colonnades, physically embracing the Square - and symbolically all those who gather there. Designed and built by Bernini between 1656 and 1657, they consist of four rows of 284 columns in the Doric style. They in turn support an entablature with an array of statues of 140 saints. The whole presents a perfect feeling of space and grace. For those interested in the mathematics of ellipses and optical illusions should stand on one of the two marble discs close to the obelisk and watch the four rows of columns disappear into just one row. It is also a lovely place to sprawl, and laze in the sun, and literally watch the world go by, whilst taking in the magnificent sights and sounds of this great Square and Basilica.

St Peter's today

My feeling on my very first visit was of being in a large, bustling rail terminus, rather than a tranquil place of worship. But, on reflection, and with a conscious removal of selfishness and the feeling of self righteousness, I returned with an air of calm determination and detachment. Taking one's time, being systematic, and having a good guide book was the key: I recommend the Vatican book '*St Peter's Guide to the Square and Basilica*' - it is beautifully illustrated, easy to follow and one is not overwhelmed with detail - and you can go at your own pace. St Peter's is a sumptuous banquet to be slowly savoured and digested, and not, as the modern world would have it, a fast food snack! By the end of my self-conducted tour, I felt very much at peace - I had fallen in love with St Peter's.

There are three major areas of St Peter's to explore and savour - which I can describe simply as: above ground, ground level, and below ground.

GROUND LEVEL

Baldacchino and Confessio

Ground level starts at the entrance portico - itself the size of any self-respecting cathedral - and once inside, the central nave, side aisles and transepts. On entering at the rear of the central nave, one's eye is immediately drawn down its length to the huge edifice of Bernini's bronze *baldacchino*, standing at the intersection of the nave and transepts, twisting gracefully upwards and exuding a heady combination of power and elegance, and itself dwarfed by the majestic dome immediately above. Beneath the *baldacchino* is the papal altar, carved from a massive block of white Greek marble, at which only the Pope celebrates Mass. Immediately in front of the altar is the *Confessio*, below which St Peter's earthly remains have been laid to rest, and to which every pilgrim is drawn and has come to venerate.

However, before moving down the nave to the *Confessio*, cast an eye left or right to the nave's side wall on which are the holy water stoups - those functional vessels at the entrance to every Catholic church - and note that the seemingly diminutive cherubs holding up these stoups are actually two metres high, giving another clue of the scale of things to come in the Basilica!

Confession of Faith

Once reaching the *Confessio* at ground level it will be seen that it embraces the foot of the papal altar with a horseshoe balustrade of marble, around which many of the oil lamps burn in silent prayer to the Apostle. It is here that the pilgrim can make their first act of thanksgiving and prayer by kneeling and confessing their faith. (This act of reverence may also be done by the Apostle's tomb in the *sacellum* below - see below p. 56).

Meditation
Whilst there are no factual accounts of Peter's martyrdom, Sienkiewicz, in his book 'Quo Vadis' gives a moving picture of what this scene might have been:
'Peter was led out of the prison sometime after noon, walking in the middle of a squad of soldiers. He wasn't forced to carry his own cross; no one thought he would

be able to lift one at his age, nor was the customary wooden yoke locked round his neck. He walked alone, unbound, and his brethren could see him very well. Tears and sobbing broke out when they caught sight of his white head among the iron helmets, but their grief died quickly. The old man's face was so cheerful and untroubled, and it glowed with such immense confidence and joy, that everyone understood at once this wasn't a victim going to his execution but a conqueror marching to his triumph...And no one there (at the execution site), neither the digging soldiers nor the gathered Christians, guessed or realised that a real king of Rome was standing among them. Caesars would come and go, waves of barbarians would sweep down and then vanish, and ages would go by, but this old man would rule here without a moment's pause'.

From the Second Letter of St Peter:

That is why I will always go on recalling the same truths to you, even though you already know them and are firmly fixed in these truths. I am sure it is my duty, as long as I am in this tent, to keep stirring you up with reminders, since I know the time for me to lay aside this tent is coming soon, as our Lord Jesus Christ made clear to me. And I shall take great care that after my own departure you will still have a means to recall these things to mind. (1:12-15)

Prayer

Lord God Almighty, I give you thanks and praise and glory for leading me to this most holy place where your First Shepherd on Earth gave his final, earthly witness with the ultimate sacrifice of his life. We thank you for his lasting witness through your Word. In meditating on these words, we ask for his intercession as we boldly proclaim that same witness, and in so doing pray that You strengthen us in faith.

(A confession of Faith may now follow, ie the Apostle's Creed).

Two broad, shallow, marble staircases (not accessible to the public) lead down from the *Confessio* to the lower level of the *sacellum*, of which more on the section 'below ground'.

You are Peter

From the area of the *baldacchino* one can now gaze up at the great dome, richly adorned with mosaics and stucco decoration, 233 feet in circumference and 394 feet from floor to roof. Prominent are the four spandrels depicting the four Evangelists, and above them, around the base of the dome's drum we can read the black letters, six feet high: "*Tu es Petrus et super hanc petram aedificabo ecclesiam meam et tibi dabo claves regni caelorum*" ("You are Peter and on this rock I will build my Church, to you I will give the keys of the kingdom of heaven" (*Mt* 16:18-19). Right at the very top of the dome, in the crown of the lantern, surveying the whole scene below in majesty, is the glorious figure of God the Father.

Having venerated the Saint at his tomb, the next thing the pilgrim may consider is paying respects, in the traditional manner of all pilgrims, by pausing at the bronze statue of St Peter in the central nave, and with a short personal prayer or salutation, touching or kissing his right foot, now worn shapeless to a soft, mellow patina by those millions of fellow pilgrims who have filed passed.

The Pieta

A detailed tour of the Basilica can now start. There is a wealth of riches to wonder at and ponder over. I can only offer you a handful, you will no doubt discover many more. Starting on the right, just where you first entered, is the Chapel of the Pieta, where Michelangelo's statue, carved from a single block of white Carrara marble, depicts a serenely sorrowful - and accepting - Virgin Mary, gently embracing her lifeless Son. It is a powerful portrayal of life and death - and of hope yet to be realised. Intriguingly, Michelangelo chose not to represent the wounds of the Crucifixion on the dead Christ.

The Pieta (Michelangelo), St Peter's Basilica.

Prayer

O Mary, Mother of Mercy, watch over all people, that the Cross of Christ may not be emptied of its power, that man may not stray from the path of the good or become blind to sin, but may put his hope ever more fully in God who is rich in mercy". (Pope John Paul II, *Veritatis Splendor*)

Blessed Sacrament

Moving on, anti-clockwise, one comes to the Chapel of the Blessed Sacrament, where, through heavy curtains one can seek some solace and quiet from the busy hum of the Basilica with a period of Adoration of Jesus in the Blessed Sacrament. The glorious decoration of the chapel reflects the importance of it being a place of Adoration. Most striking is the gilded bronze tabernacle by Bernini, flanked by two exquisite bronze angels gazing on in adulation, the whole looked down on by a powerful portrayal of the Holy Trinity - a small point of interest being that this is the only canvas in the Basilica, all the other pictures are mosaics, made up of the tiniest fragments, detectable only from close up, but creating the most exquisite and fine detail.

Prayer

Lord Jesus, stay with us! Sustain us in our weariness, forgive our sins and direct our steps on the path of goodness... In the Eucharist you made yourself the 'medicine of immortality': give us the taste for a full life

that will help us journey on as trusting and joyful pilgrims on this earth, our gaze fixed on the goal of life without end. Stay with us, Lord! Stay with us!"
(Pope John Paul II, *Mane Nobiscum Dominum*).

John XXIII

Moving on down from the Blessed Sacrament Chapel, and possibly drawn by an obvious, larger gathering of pilgrims round this point, is the tomb of Blessed John XXIII, recently relocated from the Grottoes below ground, and now movingly visible in the glass fronted tomb, in his full papal regalia. It was John, of peasant stock, with the blunt, robust and pragmatic nature, who, despite being regarded as a '*Papa di passagio*', a caretaker Pope, at the age of 77 had the gifted vision and drive to convene the Second Vatican Council in October 1962. The Council was designed to catch up, and keep pace with the modern world; a Council of renewal, to make the Faith 'more Catholic and less Roman'; and to foster Christian unity - to embrace, in his words, 'our separated brethren'. The outcome was not without its controversies, but nonetheless shaped the direction of the Catholic faith for the twenty first century. John died in June 1963, and it was his successor, Paul VI, who brought the Council to conclusion in 1965.

Relics

Passing again through the central area under the dome, one will study the four huge statues overlooking the Loggia of the Relics, all associated with holy relics that are, or have been lodged in the Basilica - St Longinus, the soldier who pierced the side of Christ; St Helen, Constantine's mother; St Veronica, who wiped Jesus' face with her veil; and the Apostle, St Andrew. On a practical note, it is through doors at the foot of these piers that give access to below ground - the Vatican Grottoes - usually the one below that of St Longinus. Also, when moving down the central nave and transepts, it is worth looking up at the niches and keeping track of the 39 statues of the founders of various religious Orders. Access to the right transept is usually limited, the area being reserved for the Sacrament of Reconciliation, being heard in the many languages of the world.

Throne

Having gone beyond the dome area to the far end of the Basilica, one's focus now rests on the Altar of the Chair in the centre of the apse. It is a glorious work by Bernini, the centre piece being the gilded bronze throne that encases an ancient wooden chair said to be that on which St Peter sat. The throne is suspended on golden clouds, surrounded by four Doctors of the Church and other symbols of the Pontiff's authority. A joyful, tumbling tumult of angels and seraphs, billowing clouds and golden amber-rays all surround a blazing window centred on the Dove of the Holy Spirit hovering above the Chair.

Alexander

One of the monuments that had a big impact - in the passage between the apse and the left transept - was that of Alexander VII. Apart from what the memorial depicts in all its detail, it was to me the most amazing demonstration of how something so solid and unyielding as marble (in this instance Sicilian jasper) is transformed into the soft pliable material of the huge billowing drapes over the doorway below, that you almost feel you can pick up and fold! There is also a sad little detail that will wring the hearts of English Catholics - the statue of Truth places her foot on the world, but very precisely on England. It was Alexander VII who instigated, approved and encouraged Bernini in his design of the Altar of the Chair and the design of St Peter's Square. It is fitting that this dramatic memorial to him was created by Bernini, being his last work, aged 80.

Presentation

And then way back round almost to the entrance of the Basilica again, in the left side-aisle is the Chapel of the Presentation of the Virgin Mary at the Temple, where a beautiful mosaic by Romanelli shows the child Mary being given over by her parents, Joachim and Anna, to service in the temple. Even taking into account the highly artistic and romanticised depiction of this event, it still strikes a deep chord, that Mary, even at that age, was completely accepting and trusting in the Lord's plans for her; a poignant contrast, but with a similar resonance, to the Pieta scene in the Chapel nearly opposite on the other side.

Benedict XV

On the left wall of the Presentation Chapel is the monument to Benedict XV, where it is worth pausing and pondering over one of the reasons that John Paul II's successor, Benedict XVI, consciously chose this name: "I wanted to be called Benedict XVI in order to create a spiritual bond with Benedict XV, who steered the Church through the period of turmoil caused by the First World War. He was a courageous and authentic prophet of peace, and strove with brave courage first of all to avert the tragedy of the war and then to limit its harmful consequences. Treading his footsteps, I would like to place my ministry at the service of reconciliation and harmony between persons and peoples, since I am profoundly convinced that the great good of peace is first and foremost a gift of God, a precious but unfortunately fragile gift to pray for, safeguard and build up, day after day, with the help of all".

Stuarts

My last treasure before leaving the main Basilica is close
to the Presentation Chapel - the Monument to the Stuarts.
Commissioned by the British Government and paid for
by King George III on its completion in 1821, it
commemorates James III (1688-1766) Pretender to the
throne, and his two sons, Charles the Duke - Bonny
Prince Charlie - and Cardinal Henry Stuart, the last
members of the Stuart line. All three had been exiled to
Rome, where they died. The end of this family line is
portrayed by two mournful angels on each side of closed
doors, gently extinguishing the flames from their
upturned torches.

BELOW GROUND

The Vatican Grottoes

Below ground level - at the level of the old St Peter's -
are the Vatican grottoes. The mortal remains of 148
Popes lie within the Basilica, and it is down here that
many reside. There is also on display much evidence -
from the modern excavations beneath the Basilica - from
the Rome of the previous millennia: monuments,
mosaics, sculptures, pagan and Christian tombs. It was
during these excavations, ordered by Pius XII in 1939,
that archaeologists from the University of Rome

discovered a chest of bones and fragments of garments that, with corroborating graffiti, other documentary evidence and scientific testing, led Pope Paul VI in 1968 to solemnly declare that truly the remains of St Peter the Apostle had been found.

And it is here, that the pilgrim, through an archway declaring '*Sepulcrum Sancti Petri Apostoli*', can view the *sacellum*, directly underneath the *Confessio* and papal altar, and under which the Apostle's remains rest. The *sacellum* is flanked by statues of Ss Peter and Paul, and at the centre, in the *sacellum* niche, one can view the bronze casket that contains the *pallia* - the narrow white stoles woven from the wool of lambs and blessed on the feast of St Agnes (a patron Saint of Rome) (21 January). These stoles are embroidered with black crosses and bestowed by the Pope on patriarchs and metropolitan archbishops as a symbol of Christ the Good Shepherd and symbolising 'one flock'.

Papal Tombs

The most recent addition to the papal tombs in the Grottoes is that of Pope John Paul II, the 264th Shepherd of Christ, the first non-Italian for nearly half a millennium: philosopher, author, poet, linguist - and world leader. He was 'the pilgrim Pope', the most widely travelled of Popes, who understood the power of promoting and maintaining the visibility of the Church in the modern world - and not only in spiritual matters, but also on the world political scene. Astute politician, he was largely instrumental, in his blunt defence of the Polish Solidarity movement and outright condemnation of communism, in the eventual downfall of the communist monolith. He was no less sparing on the corrosive effects of capitalism. In the words of one commentator, "This was not a Pope who looked at public opinion polls. He said what he thought was right and wrong from conviction. And that's why people admired him, he was a man of integrity and prayer, even if they did not agree with him". His legacy to Catholicism, Christianity, and the world at large was immense, and the pilgrim can give heartfelt thanks for this holy man of God as they file past his simple but eloquent tomb - this man, whose soul is elevated to the heights of the Heavenly Host, but whose mortal remains lie humbly - as he was humble - at ground level.

Prayer

O God, we give you thanks for the precious gift of your faithful servant John Paul. By his example may we strive to follow, by his witness may we strive to live, by his love of humanity and all life may we strive to love. We give you thanks for his strength, courage, wisdom and conviction, his total devotion to Your Mother, and his total giving of himself to You. And in his words we pray, "To you crucified Jesus, the wisdom and the power of God be honour and glory for ever and ever". Amen.

ABOVE GROUND

The Dome

To climb the dome, and view Rome, is a must. Get there early to avoid the crowds. A lift takes one part of the way, but there are many steps to be climbed to reach the top. The effort is well worth it. The first indication as to the immensity of it all is when one emerges on the circular balcony high up, inside the base of the dome, and where one's eyes immediately plunge down into the heart of the Basilica overlooking the *baldacchino* and the cross naves. The contrasting scales of the tiny people below and the huge lettering close to you round the base of the dome gives a good perspective of scale. One can only marvel at the sheer design and engineering as you negotiate the staircase round the side of the curving wall of the dome itself. On emerging into daylight just under the pinnacle, the views are stunning. St Peter's Square laid out below with the ant-like people, unparalleled views of the Roman vista and its sky line, and a remarkable outlook over the Vatican City and gardens.

One other bonus, which I did not realise before I went up, was the existence, on the roof of the Basilica and in the immediate shadow of the dome, of a small cafe, gift shop and toilets. After the exertions of climbing the dome, there was nothing more pleasant than lazing in the

sun on the roof of Rome, with a cup of coffee, viewing
the scurrying ant-like world below!

How to sum up St Peter's!? The sheer majesty of the
place - the Basilica and the Square - down to the smallest
exquisite detail, will beguile, intrigue and inform you;
this great physical and beautiful rock, from which the
Universal Church emanates and is governed by the
current, direct successor to Peter, will inspire you; that
the Rock of the Church - Peter, and his many, many
successors - rest here, will give you that timeless,
unbroken physical link back to Jesus, Our Lord; the sight
of those many thousand fellow pilgrims, drawn here from
all corners of the earth and visibly representing the
Universal Church, makes this extraordinary meeting
place the physical confluence of the world-wide Catholic
Church - a Church built not of stone, but of people.

> *How good, how delightful it is*
> *to live as brothers all together!*
> (*Ps* 133:1)

❧ OUR LADY IN ROME ❧

ST MARY MAJOR

Devotees of Our Lady are completely spoilt for choice - there being upwards of sixty churches dedicated to her in Rome. The most prominent is St Mary Major, also known as the Church of the Snows, one of the four patriarchal basilicas of Rome. The legend of its conception and location comes from the tradition that a wealthy Roman citizen, praying to Our Lady to further grace his life, had a dream that he should build a church in her honour in the area where snow would fall that August day in the year 352. Thinking this highly unlikely, he nonetheless reported his dream to the Pope, Liberius, who with great surprise had experienced the same dream that night. On being told that snow had fallen that day, they went to the spot on the summit of the Esquiline Hill, and the Pope, with his crosier, scratched out in the snow the outline of a huge basilica that he envisaged being dedicated to Our Lady.

However, historical research reveals that the present basilica was probably not started before 420, possibly over the remains of any church built during Liberius' time. Its conception and construction was linked to reinforce and proclaim Mary as Mother of God, as

declared at the Council of Ephesus (431). The charm of
the legend is not forgotten though - because on the 5
August every year a special Mass is celebrated in the
Pauline chapel, in which, during the consecration,
thousands of white petals fall from the ceiling.

I have in my mind's eye an image of glittering gold as
I looked up at the sumptuous and intricate detail of the
gilded, Renaissance coffered ceiling, of a majestic
procession of the forty Ionic pink marble columns
leading to the high altar, the mosaics of Old Testament
themes above each column, and on moving through,
hardly daring to walk on the twelfth century Cosmati
pavement of inlaid marble patterns. The whole centres-in
on the handsome *baldacchino* of red porphyry and
bronze, and accompanying *confessio*, and in the apse
beyond, a graceful mosaic of the crowning of Our Lady
as Queen of Heaven, and below it, other scenes from the
life of Our Lady.

Pauline Chapel

In being selective, I concentrated my efforts on the
gorgeous Pauline side chapel - the Chapel of the Snows.
Above the altar is an ancient image of the Madonna,
painted by an unknown Byzantine artist of apostolic
times, but traditionally attributed to St Luke. Beneath it is
the inscription '*Salus populi Romani*', 'Salvation of the
Roman People'. One commentator, so taken by the

beauty of this chapel, was moved to write, "Unless words were gems that would flame with many coloured lights upon the page, and thence throw a tremendous glimmer into the reader's eyes, it were vain to attempt a description of this princely chapel".

Prayer

Mary, Mother of hope, accompany us on our journey! Teach us to proclaim the living God; help us to bear witness to Jesus, the one Saviour; make us kindly towards our neighbours, welcoming to the needy, concerned for justice, impassioned builders of a more just world; intercede for us as we carry out your work in history, certain that the Father's plan will be fulfilled.

(John Paul II, *Ecclesia in Europa*)

FOUR HISTORICAL MARIAN CHURCHES

In wanting to take you to some other lovely churches to venerate Our Lady, I also want to serve the dual purpose of informing those with a historical and architectural bent by guiding you through a time-line of Rome through the ages. Apart from their beauty, there are four churches I have in mind: the medieval church (12th century) of St Mary in Trastevere, Gothic (13th century) at St Mary's over Minerva (Santa Maria sopra Minerva), early Renaissance (15th century) of St Mary of the People (Santa Maria del

Popolo), and the Baroque (17th century) of St Mary of the
Victory (Santa Maria del Vittoria), all of them unique and
memorable in their own way.

St Mary in Trastevere

The particular draw to St Mary in Trastevere is twofold.
Firstly, Our Lady has been venerated here since earliest
times. Secondly, it is recognised as the church where the
first acts of Christian worship 'officially' took place in
Rome in the early third century, before Christianity was
'legalised' by Constantine in the fourth century. In effect
it is the first 'parish church', in Rome, possibly in
Christendom. It gives one a sense of timelessness and
continuity, and a feeling of stability and hope in one's
faith when praying in this church, particularly having in
mind one's own parishioners, parish priest and parish
church. From this church there is also a direct link back
to the catacombs of St Callistus, as it stands on the site of
Callistus' house used as a house church (*titulus Callisti*)
in those early times.

Today's church, rebuilt in the twelfth century, sits
modestly back in a corner of the piazza named after it.
There was a jolly Italian wedding party gathered outside
when I visited, giving it the stamp of a living, breathing
church, embracing the local community. The church is
particularly renowned for its twelfth century mosaics,
both on the façade, but more strikingly, a glorious

depiction in glittering gold and vibrant colours in the bowl of the apse, of Jesus and Mary enthroned, surrounded by the saints. The most venerated image in the church is the 6/7th century icon of the Madonna of Mercy in the Altemps side chapel. Despite some Baroque additions in the eighteenth century, this charming church retains much of its original medieval character.

Meditation

It is Mary's prerogative to be the Morning Star, which heralds in the sun. She does not shine for herself, but she is the reflection of her and our Redeemer, and she glorifies Him. When she appears in the darkness, we know that He is close at hand. (Cardinal John Henry Newman)

Santa Maria sopra Minerva

This church also had early origins: as its name spells out, the first church (and convent) was built over the ruins of the Temple to Minerva, the pagan goddess of war in the late eighth century. The present church, one of the very few examples of Gothic architecture in Rome, was built by the Dominicans in the 13th century. Its arched and vaulted surrounds reflect the importance of this church in its time, with the many sumptuous aristocratic side chapels and the extraordinary wealth of its artistic patrimony. There is a wide range of Italian art going through the ages, most prominent of which is a powerful statue of the Resurrected Christ by Michelangelo. Five Popes are buried here, and under the high altar rests the body of St Catherine of Siena (see p. 92, Saints in Rome). An interesting link with this church to England and Wales is that the current Cardinal Archbishop of Westminster, Cardinal Cormac Murphy O'Connor, is the Cardinal-Priest of the title Santa Maria sopra Minerva. As a side note, those who want to catch Mass in English can do so at St Susanna's (the American church), the English College or San Silvestro in Capite.

Meditation
O Mary, Mary, Temple of the Trinity, O Mary, carrier of fire, Mary distributor of mercy. Mary, who makes the Divine Fruit germinate! Mary, redemptress, in one sense, of the human race! (The suffering of your flesh in the Word, did it not save the world?) Christ was Redeemer by His Passion; you by the suffering of body and soul.
(St Catherine of Siena)

Santa Maria del Popolo

This is a most exquisite church. It is small, but through the most perfect use of symmetry and space, it creates an illusion of size. No wonder, as among the contributing architects and artists were Bramante, Raphael and Bernini. In terms of architectural wonder, I was drawn to the diminutive Chigi side chapel by

Raphael, topped with a beautiful, minute dome - it is stunning. This tiny chapel gives the feeling of a glorious, soaring cathedral. In artistic terms in the church there are two very dramatic, vibrant pictures by Caravaggio, the drama being heightened by their very striking perspectives. One is the Conversion of St Paul, showing a dazed and stunned young man in complete disarray, having fallen off his horse; the second is the Crucifixion of St Peter, in which one can be totally immersed in the pain and shock being experienced by the old man, as well as note the workaday expressions and attitudes of his executioners.

Santa Maria del Popolo is one of the first Renaissance churches to be built in Rome, commissioned by Pope Sixtus IV in 1472, and as its name implies, financed by the people of Rome.

Meditation

Let us seek to rest ever closer, each day, to the Immaculate One; in this way we will become ever closer to the Heart of Jesus, of God the Father, of the whole of the Most Holy Trinity, because no other creature is closer to the Divinity than the Immaculate One. And in this way also we will draw all those who are close to our heart closer to the Immaculate One and to the good God.

(Saint Maximillian Kolbe)

Santa Maria della Vittoria

In contrast to Santa Maria del Popolo, this small, rich, Baroque church is completely overwhelming, having a dizzying, kaleidoscopic effect, with every square inch - floor to ceiling - being painted, sculpted, gilded or patterned - a feeling of space closing in on one. It is spectacular, and it is just glorious! The church was built by the Discalced Carmelites between 1608 and 1620 over the site of a previous chapel dedicated to St Paul. History has it that the church's name commemorates the victory of the inferior Catholic League army, who, inspired by their chaplain carrying an image of Our Lady and the infant Jesus into battle, routed the superior Lutheran army, near Prague in 1620. This image is displayed in the church, as is a painting of the chaplain, the Ven P Domenico of Jesus and Mary, a Discalced Carmelite.

Everything about this church is sumptuous and beautiful, down to the last glittering detail. Each of the eight side chapels is worth a good scrutiny - thankfully, the church is small enough to allow this extravagance! And in a strange realisation of the new meeting the old, many of these chapels are dedicated to the patron saints of Youth 2000, a young vibrant, international organisation of the Church of today founded in England - St Therese of the Child Jesus, St Francis of Assisi, and St Joseph. (see CTS booklet *Youth 2000*)

But by far the most dramatic and famous of statues in this church, and indeed in the Church - is that of the Ecstasy of St Teresa of Jesus (and of Avila). And, yes, one has got to point out that it was designed by the prodigious Bernini! It is a statue that conveys and evokes a wide range of emotions, taken by Bernini from St Teresa's description of her ecstatic experience. It expresses an exquisite tension between spiritual ecstasy and earthly sensuality - a theme much emphasised in 17th century devotion - and this powerful, dynamic work can be viewed and interpreted in many ways:

"Beside me on the left appeared an angel in bodily form ... He was not tall but short, and very beautiful; and his face was so aflame that he appeared to be one of the highest ranks of angels, who seem to be all on fire ... In his hands I saw a great golden spear, and at the iron tip there appeared to be a point of fire. This he plunged into my heart several times so that it penetrated my entrails. When he pulled it out I felt that he took them with it, and left me utterly consumed by the great love of God. The pain was so severe that it made me utter several moans. The sweetness caused by this intense pain is so extreme that one can not possibly wish it to cease, nor is one's soul content with anything but God. This is not a physical but a spiritual pain, though the body has some share in it - even a considerable share."

The Crucifixion of St Peter (Caravaggio), Santa Maria del Popolo.

Bizarrely, the whole scene is looked down on from each side, in theatre style, by statues of seven cardinals and a Doge, all members of the Cornaro family, for whom the statue was sculpted.

Prayer

Hail, O holy Lady, most holy Queen, Mary, mother of God, ever Virgin, chosen from heaven on high by the Father most holy, consecrated by Him and by His most holy and beloved Son and by the comforting Spirit, you in whom has been and is to be found the fullness of grace and all goodness. Hail to you His tabernacle. Hail to you His abode. Hail to you His Mother, and to you all, O holy virtues, who, by the grace and the light of the Holy Spirit, are poured into the hearts of the faithful, that from unfaithfulness they may be brought to faithfulness to God. (Saint Francis of Assisi)

Madonelle

There are many other signs throughout Rome of the enduring love that the Romans have of Our Lady, and on becoming conscious of them they are not difficult to spot, always with a certain amount of delight, wherever one goes. These are in the form of many hundreds of *Madonelle*, statuettes of Our Lady, gracing niches on the front of buildings and street corners, from the humble and unadorned, probably put up by a family, to the more ornate and elaborate, possibly put up by a grateful local community, because underneath there often appears the letters PGR, *per grazie ricevute*, thanks for favours received.

Prayer - The Memorare

Remember, O most loving Virgin Mary, that it is a thing unheard of, that anyone ever had recourse to your protection, implored your help, or sought your intercession, and was left forsaken.

Filled therefore with confidence in your goodness I fly to you, O Mother, Virgin of virgins. To you I come, before you I stand, a sorrowful sinner. Despise not my poor words, O Mother of the Word of God, but graciously hear and grant my prayer.

The Mother of God is a model of the Church in the matter of faith, charity and perfect union with Christ
(*Lumen Gentium*, 23).

∽ PILGRIMAGE TO THE ∽
SEVEN CHURCHES

A book on the pilgrimage to the seven churches published in 1694 describes it as 'a pilgrimage peradventure the most celebrated after Calvary and the Sepulchre of Christ', and is an old medieval tradition that was revived and promoted by St Philip Neri (see section on the Saints in Rome p. 95) in the sixteenth century. In his day, he and his followers would start at St Peter's, walking south to St Paul's Outside the Walls beyond the city outskirts, and then across to the Tomb of St Sebastian on the old Appian Way, back into the city to St John Lateran, up a short way to the Holy Cross in Jerusalem, heading out again to St Lawrence Outside the Walls, before finally ending back in the city at St Mary Major. To the modern pilgrim this could be an exhaust-fumed and exhausting challenge considering the extensive urbanisation of Rome since those days. All are accessible by taxi, tram, bus or Metro!

This section takes in those churches along this pilgrim route that are not already mentioned in other parts of this book, namely, St Peter's (see p. 40) and St Mary Major (see p. 60).

St Paul's Outside the Walls

Two things immediately struck me about St Paul's. The first was quite how 'ordinary' a building it looked on approaching it from the side, however, one that is dispelled when you get round to the front. But once inside, there was an explosion of space and a presentation of clean lines, created by its sheer loftiness and 'airiness' with the wide, pillared nave and open, double aisles each side, and also by the absence of the clutter of any side chapels in the main nave, so predominant, and potentially distracting, in the many other churches. However, a bit of history first. The story of St Paul is well known - the great Apostle to the Gentiles, who, after his travels was brought to Rome under arrest in AD 61, and his imprisonment for two years, during which he wrote his celebrated letters. He was acquitted of the charges against him, but in AD 64, after the great fire of Rome, he was arrested by Nero as one of the instigators, incarcerated in the Mamertine jail, and in AD 67, was martyred by beheading at Aqua Salviae (Three Fountains), outside the Aurelian walls.

Destruction and Restoration

Despite Christianity being outlawed in those early times, a small *memoriae* was built over his tomb, and became, over the years, a place of pilgrimage and veneration. As with St Peter, it was Constantine who commissioned a simple place of worship to be built, which was subsequently developed by successive Emperors into an imposing basilica, consecrated by Pope Siricius in 390. Over the centuries, as with many churches and buildings in Rome, it underwent cycles of destruction and restoration - it being particularly vulnerable outside the protective walls of Rome. However, in1823 this splendid basilica was almost completely destroyed by fire, and the painful, and costly task of rebuilding began, reinterpreting as faithfully as possible the original. Although work continued for many years beyond, the new Basilica was consecrated by Pope Pius IX in 1854.

St Paul

One enters the Basilica, through a magnificent colonnade, into a large, imposing atrium, and is immediately faced with a dominant, hooded and stern statue of St Paul, grimly clutching a sword, the instrument of his martyrdom. High above, on the church façade, there are large, vibrant mosaics, one with Jesus, flanked by Ss Peter and Paul, underneath, a peaceful pastoral scene depicting the Lamb of God on the mountain of Paradise. Below that stand four Old Testament prophets.

On entering the central nave, one's eye sweeps down the magnificent parade of the granite columns upholding the arches, down to the original thirteenth century canopy, underneath which is the *confessio*, where the Apostle's remains rest, and it is here that one can meditate and pray.

Meditations

As with St Peter, there is no record of Paul's execution. In his book, 'Quo Vadis', Seinkiewicz pictures it thus: He went on, joyful and at peace, like a labourer who has worked hard in the fields all day and hurries home at sunset. His thoughts like Peter's, were as calm and clear as the evening sky.... He recalled his journeys, hardships, work and struggles; he remembered all the churches he had founded in so many lands and beyond the seas, and counted his victories; he thought he had done enough to earn his rest...He was going to his reward like a conqueror... Yes, the hour had come... He repeated to himself the words he had written earlier in his cell, conscious of his work's completion and his approaching end: I've fought the good fight. I have run my course. I have kept the faith. The crown of righteousness waits for me in heaven" (cf 2 Tm 4:7-8).

St Paul suggests to each pilgrim to let himself or herself be evangelised and, even more, to understand the importance of being an evangeliser. The Christian, amid the crisis of civilisation, is called to contribute towards a culture of love, founded on universal values of peace, solidarity, justice and freedom. 'There should be no more postponement of the time when the poor Lazarus can sit beside the rich man to share the same banquet and be forced no more to feed on the scraps that fall from the table'. (Vatican Guide for the Jubilee Year 2000)

Prayer

Almighty God, as I kneel before your faithful Apostle, Paul, I ask for Your grace to recognise those occasions when evangelisation is being offered to me, and not to turn them away or spurn them, but to willingly open my mind and heart to receive and accept them. Give me also the courage to become an evangeliser, at the very least by being able to give silent witness by living the Gospel life of love. In this extreme culture of 'self', help me - in humility and charity - to share those riches, in whatever form you give me, with the poor Lazarus. Amen.

Chapels

In this vast church there are many items to ponder over. Running in a band, along all the walls, are individual and sequential mosaic medallions of every Pope, from St Peter to John Paul II, providing a fascinating, unbroken visual history of the Church, which is quite unique. Above these, in the nave and transepts, are 36 frescoes depicting St Paul's life. In a lovely touch symbolising God's reconciliation between enemies, is a side chapel in one of the transepts to St Stephen, the first martyr of the Church, at whose martyrdom Paul was present as a persecutor of Christians. In the Blessed Sacrament Chapel hangs a 14th century Crucifix from which tradition has it, the head of Christ inclined itself to St

Bridget in 1370 as she knelt before it, deep in prayer. Also in the Chapel is a somewhat battered and splintered wooden statue of St Paul, having suffered from relic hunting pilgrims! There is also a fine 13th mosaic of the Madonna and Child, in front of which, in 1541, St Ignatius of Loyola, the founder of the Society of Jesus (the Jesuits) knelt when taking his vows.

In the right hand transept, near the canopy, stands an intricately carved 12th century marble candlestick, charged with religious symbolism, and standing well over fifteen feet high, used from the Middle Ages to hold the Paschal candle on Holy Saturday. Very striking, at the ends of the transepts, are the two vivid green malachite altars donated by Czar Nicholas I, which contrast vibrantly with the browns, creams and greys of the patterned marble that they back onto. Having feasted visually and spiritually in this great banquet hall, there is the opportunity to come down a gear or two by resting in the serene 13th century cloister adjacent to the Basilica.

THE BASILICA OF ST SEBASTIAN

Soldier and Martyr

Away from the immediate buzz and rumble of the city, by the side of the Old Appian Way in tranquil greenery, stands the church and catacombs of St Sebastian. In the early days of the Church Ss Peter and Paul were venerated here by those probably fearful of being seen in the more public places of the Vatican Hill and Via Ostensis where the Apostles were martyred. It is also possible that the Apostles' remains were temporarily interred here during times of persecution. In the fourth century Pope Julius ordered the building of a basilica on this site, dedicated to Ss Peter and Paul (*Basilica Apostolorum*). However, by the 9th century, St Peter's and St Paul's, by now being well established as places of pilgrimage, the Basilica was re-dedicated to St Sebastian, a prominent Roman soldier, who publicly turned to Christianity, and was martyred for his faith. The legend tells that he survived execution by arrows, as his martyrdom is depicted, and went back to the Emperor Diocletian to continue to plead for mercy for persecuted Christians, and for so doing, was put to death by beating and his body thrown into a sewer.

The present Basilica was started in 1608. The church nowadays is a combination of place of worship in the basilica, tourist attraction with the catacombs, and part museum, displaying many artefacts, graffiti of early times, and models of the church through its various stages of development. In the church it is worth noting the fine, carved wooden ceiling, the statue of St Sebastian, and the altar with the urn containing his remains. The Chapel of the Relics contains one of the arrows that pierced him, the column to which he was tied, and the stone said to bear the imprint of

Jesus' footprints - (see explanation above at p. 14ff). The crypt of St Sebastian with a bust of him attributed to Bernini, and the *cubiculum* of St Philip Neri, are worth viewing, as is the *triclia*, the porticoed courtyard where rites and funeral banquets in honour of Ss Peter and Paul were held, and where the scratched supplications to the Apostles in Latin and Greek are evocatively evident.

Meditation

Blessed are those who are persecuted in the cause of uprightness: the kingdom of Heaven is theirs. / Blessed are you when people abuse you and persecute you and speak all kinds of calumny against you falsely on my account. / Rejoice and be glad, for your reward will be great in Heaven; this is how they persecuted the prophets before you. (Mt 5:10-12).

ST JOHN LATERAN

The Pope's Church

St John Lateran is a great, proud monolith of a church, dominated on high from the façade, by the statue of Christ the Saviour, flanked by the other dynamic statues of Ss John the Baptist and the Evangelist, and eight Doctors of the Latin and Greek Churches. It stands out from the surrounding area, and its size is emphasised by the pleasant green tree-lined approach, and empty grassed space in front of it. In contemplating this wonderful building, Dante said of it in his Divine Comedy, "If the barbarians from the distant land coming to Rome were astonished by her great monuments, when above all of which rose the Lateran, just imagine how moved was I". Its title, given to this church alone is, 'Most holy church of the Lateran, mother and foundation of the churches of all cities and of the world', and sums up its standing as the first Christian basilica of Rome, and the world, and is the seat of the Bishop of Rome - the Pope - taking pre-eminence over all other churches. Up until the fourteenth century it was also the seat of the papacy, which subsequently moved to the Vatican on return from the Avignon exile in 1377.

It was built, once again, on the initiative of Constantine, over land belonging to the Laterani family and former horse guard barracks, between 314 and 318. It was consecrated to Christ the Saviour by Pope Silvester I in 324. This church's history accurately reflects the turbulent history of Rome, a cycle of ransack and destruction by invaders or natural occurrences, followed by rebuilding and restoration. It was twice destroyed by fire, and rebuilt. After a major rebuild in 904, Pope Sergius III added St John the Baptist as a patron; two centuries later in 1144, St John the Evangelist was named as the third co-patron, completing a symbolic continuity and link, not only in name, but from Old Testament to New, the Word being made Flesh. The Basilica's present form and shape was

executed over many years between the 16th and 18th
centuries, with Borromini presiding over the interior
architecture and design in the mid 17th century.

Impressions: high above one's head, a fantastically
gilded, ornate and embellished wooden ceiling, and, below
one's feet, a beautifully patterned and detailed Cosmati
marble floor, the overall impression and effect from which
you can only get by looking at a picture of the whole. What
I found most inspiring and memorable from this church was
the statues of the twelve Apostles flanking the main nave.

Baptistry and Holy Stairs

Also of interest is the separate octagonal Baptistry, its
splendour and size reflecting the fact that baptisms in the
early Church were only conducted by the bishop in the
cathedral; it was only much later in the 7th and 8th centuries
that baptism was perforce 'delegated' to priests in the now
growing and geographically spread parish churches, to
which the bishops visited at some stage after the event to
administer the Sacrament of Confirmation - 'confirming' the
Holy Spirit on the baptised. There is also a 13th century
arched cloister, with its graceful pairs of plain and spiralling
columns. Adjacent to the church is the Lateran palace,
former residence to the Popes, and across the plaza, the
Scala Sancta (Holy Stairs) up which Christ was said to have
ascended to his judgement before Pontius Pilate, and
brought to Rome by Helena, Constantine's mother.

Meditation
The three patrons of this Basilica are linked perfectly in time and space in St John's Gospel, when he writes movingly, as Jesus and the disciples are together with John the Baptist, who bears witness for the last time:

You yourselves can bear me out. I said, "I am not the Christ; I am the one who has been sent to go in front of him". / It is the bridegroom who has the bride; and yet the bridegroom's friend, who stands there and listens to him, is filled with joy at the bridegroom's voice. This is the joy I feel, and it is complete'. (Jn 3:28-29).

Prayer
O loving God, we hear your voice through your Word, we see it in action through your holy martyrs and saints. Help us, through understanding Your Word and living by example, to aspire to holiness, a holiness that springs from the heart, and flows through our troubled minds, washing us and refreshing us. In times when there is joy in our lives, let us give you the thanks; in times when there is sadness, let us hold fast to those joyful moments, whilst trusting You to lift our burden of sorrow. Help us above all, to apply Your Son's 'new commandment' which He left us as an enduring message at the Last Supper: "Love one another, as I have loved you. (*Jn* 15:12)

THE HOLY CROSS IN JERUSALEM

Also in sight of St John Lateran, and a short walk through a park, is the Basilica of the Holy Cross in Jerusalem, the site to which Constantine's aged mother, Helena, brought back from the Holy Land the Relics of the Christ's Passion. The present church, in the care of the Cistercians since 1561, was remodelled on the Baroque style under Pope Benedict XIV's direction in the mid 18th century. One cannot help but be immediately drawn, up the wide, shallow steps and contemplating the bronze Stations of the Cross on the ascent, to the Chapel of the Relics. This modern (1952) chapel of muted marble focuses one's attention on the glass and gold reliquary on the altar, beneath a simple marble canopy. Displayed in their precious and intricate containers are the Relics: a fragment of the True Cross, a Nail of the Crucifixion, the Sign over Jesus' Cross (*Titulus*), thorns from the Crown of Thorns, the finger of St Thomas the Apostle, some stone fragments, and part of the Cross of the Good Thief.

On gazing on these Relics, and in trying to attenuate to what they are and mean, Mr Sceptical popped into my mind, and I turned to the Cistercian Brother by my side and asked how we knew that these were actually the Relics, had they been carbon dated and scientifically proved? He looked at me in a gentle, understanding way,

"That's not the point..." he said, and before he could finish, the realisation just flooded over me, and in my mind I completed the words which he went on to say, "...anything that draws us closer to Christ, particularly that which helps us focus on His Passion, will have achieved its purpose".

Meditation

How often, on hearing the Passion of Christ being spoken of, or speaking of it myself...have I repeated to myself the well known verse of Dante Alighieri: 'What do we weep at, if you do not weep at this?' The mistake is that we unconsciously think of the Passion as something that happened two thousand years ago and which belongs to the past. How can we be moved and weep over something that took place two thousand years ago? Suffering touches us when we see it, not when we remember it. We can only contemplate Christ's suffering as contemporaries, and we have it from reliable sources that 'Christ's Passion is prolonged to the end of time', and that, 'Jesus will be in agony even to the end of the world'. Scripture itself says that those who sin 'crucify the Son of God on their own account and hold him up to contempt' (Heb 6:6).

(Father Raniero Cantalamessa OFM Cap)

ST LAWRENCE OUTSIDE THE WALLS

In a way, after the dazzling splendour of Renaissance and Baroque that prevail over the churches of Rome, it was quite a relief to get to St Lawrence. On first sight, the impression of the church and its immediate surrounds, is one of a rustic transplant right into the unforgiving sights and sounds of the surrounding cityscape. Of course, it happened the other way round, with the unremitting advance of the city on this part of the countryside. The first clue on seeing St Lawrence, set well back from the piazza, is its immediate surrounds of green pines enhancing the pastoral look of the church, with its simple lines, warm red bricks and tiled roof - a restful, calming scene. The feeling is confirmed on entering - a spacious, plain unadorned church, no stained glass windows, a lofty but simple timbered and beamed ceiling, no gold or glitter - just plain brickwork, stone columns and a muted mosaic floor.

Deacon and Martyr

St Lawrence was a deacon in the middle of the third century who suffered martyrdom during Emperor Valerian's persecution. When he was ordered to surrender the treasures of the church by the Emperor's officials he brought instead a procession of the sick and poor, declaring them as "Mother Church's treasures". He was beaten with whips and then put to death by roasting on a gridiron. In memory of his martyrdom a church was built over his resting place, alongside which, in the 6th century, another church was built by Pope Pellagius II. In the 13th century, under Pope Honorius III, the work of removing both apses and connecting the two churches was undertaken. Today one can see this unique 'two churches in one' from the intriguing differing levels and the centred altar, rather unusual for a church of that time. That the design of the earlier church was influenced by the form of synagogues is seen by the women's upper galleries, reflecting the make-up of the congregation in those early Christian days of a large number of Jewish converts. Once again, the pilgrim can rest in the tiny, be-flowered cloister next to the church.

Meditation
The flames that Valerian prepared did not triumph over the flames of Christian charity, because the fire that burned Lawrence externally was weaker than flames that consumed him from within' (St Leo the Great, Homilies 85, 4). Today there are other trials of our Christian faith: the convincing persuasion of the permissive life in the West; tacit assent to unjust regimes; the economic inequality that harms two thirds of mankind; silence before laws that attack life or manipulate it; scarce efforts to wipe out the great wounds caused by poverty:

forced prostitution, child labour and sexual exploitation, organ trafficking. Lawrence the deacon reminds us all to be Christ's witnesses"

(Official Vatican guide for the Jubilee Year 2000).

Prayer

Dear Lord, as we contemplate St Lawrence's concern for the injustices of the world, and the price that he willingly paid for it, we humbly ask that we too are given the grace and strength to contribute in many more ways than we feel able. At times we feel so helpless with our seeming inability to influence the application of Your justice in the world. Reassure us, Lord, that however feeble our efforts may seem to us, you will take them, sanctify them and use them to Your purpose in a way that we may never know or recognise. To these injustices, we pledge our time, our resources, our effort, and when these seemingly run dry - may we always give that most powerful and free gift - our prayers. Amen.

The weary pilgrim in medieval times, or on St Philip Neri's pilgrimage, would now turn his footsteps, and his prayers, to the last leg of the journey - back into the city, to the final place of prayer and reflection - the Basilica of St Mary Major (see p. 60, Our Lady in Rome).

❧ THE SAINTS IN ROME ❧

There are many, many saints directly associated with Rome. For a start there are 77 Popes who have been canonised, and whose remains and memorials are placed in the basilicas, churches and catacombs in and around the city. The list spans the millennia of the Church's history. There is quite naturally, a wealth of holy men and women in the early days, when the Church suffered persecution under various Roman Emperors before Constantine's conversion to Christianity in the 4th century. Subsequent periods of strife and turbulence throughout the centuries similarly produced great men and women whose example in living, or defending their faith, have been recognised by the Church as worthy of beatification or canonisation.

The last 300 years may have seen a diminution of saints emanating from Rome, but this merely reflects where the emphasis of the Church's efforts have gone elsewhere in the world in spreading the Gospel message. There is a rich legacy left behind by those sung, and unsung, in whose footsteps we may follow with some awe and thanksgiving. Below is a small selection for those who may wish to trace these steps of our 'friends and fellow heirs of Jesus Christ, who are also our brothers and extraordinary benefactors' (*Lumen Gentium* 50), by visiting the churches and/or places where they stayed or lived in Rome. Many of these get scarce or no mention in the guide books on Rome.

Martyrs of England and Wales

Whilst it may seem strange to talk about British martyrs in a book about Rome, it is from the Venerable English College in Rome (the *Venerabile*) that many priests were trained and ordained and sent back to Britain during the period of Protestant persecution to keep the Catholic faith alive. The roots of the College go back to 1361, when an Englishman bought a house on the current site for use as a hospice for visiting English pilgrims. However, the need for a pilgrim hospice declined with the suppression of Catholicism in England, and its role changed to that of a seminary to train priests for the 'English Mission', the first students arriving in 1577. During this period, known as the 'heroic age', forty one priests have been recognised by the Church as having gone to martyrdom in England and Wales between 1581 and 1679, with a further hundred and thirty who suffered imprisonment or exile. Of the forty one: ten are canonised as saints, twenty seven have been beatified, and the remaining four approved for veneration.

The College Church, completed in 1888, contains a wealth of detail depicting English and Welsh saints and events in the history of the Church in England and Wales. Above the altar hangs a very dramatic Picture of the

Martyrs, showing the blood of the crucified Christ falling
on to the British Isles, and on which is inscribed the
College motto '*Ignem veni mittere in terram*' (I have
come to bring fire to the earth). The College is still going
strong today, providing future priests for ministry in
England and Wales. The Chapel is open to visitors;
formal tours of the College for groups can be made by
prior arrangement with the College.

Prayer for England

O Blessed Virgin Mary, Mother of God and our most
gentle Queen and Mother, look down in mercy upon
England thy Dowry, and upon us all who greatly hope
and trust in thee. By thee it was that Jesus, our Saviour
and our Hope, was given unto the world, and He has
given thee to us that we may hope still more. Plead for
us thy children, whom thou didst receive and accept at
the foot of the Cross, O sorrowful Mother. Intercede for
our separated brethren that with us in one true fold they
may be united to the Chief Shepherd, the Vicar of Thy
Son. Pray for us all, dear Mother, that by faith fruitful in
good works we may all deserve to see and praise God
together with thee in our heavenly home. Amen.

St Bridget of Sweden

Just round the corner from the English College, in Piazza
Farnese, is the church of St Bridget of Sweden. Birgitta

Godmarsson (1303-1373), a visionary, widow and Swedish noblewoman, felt called to Rome to work and pray for the reinstatement of the papacy to Rome from Avignon. Her prayers seemed to be answered when Urban V, the sixth Avignon Pope, seeing the need to return, came to Rome in 1367. He found the city in a worse state than he feared, and discouraged by apathy and lack of any progress, returned to Avignon in 1370, dying there soon after, seemingly fulfilling Birgitta's prophecy of his early death in not staying to fulfil his task. Birgitta, was canonised as St Bridget of Sweden in 1391. She founded the Order of the Bridgettines, of which the Mother House, and the place where she lived, are attached to the church.

This little gem of a church, built by a Swedish bishop in the sixteenth century, also has a distinct 'English connection' with one of its side chapels being dedicated to St Richard - Richard Reynold - a Bridgettine monk martyred in London in 1535. The attached convent is the Mother House to the Bridgettine Order of nuns, an order which also has a current English connection through the Maryvale Institute in Birmingham, where the Bridgettines supply domestic and prayer support to the Institute. This would be one of my quiet places of refuge from the bustle of the city. Adoration takes place in the church during specified hours, and if you time it right, you can join the Sisters, listening to their glorious singing and praying the

daily Liturgy. The added bonus is the opportunity to take
an informal tour of the rest of the building, being guided
by a shy, but knowledgeable Sister round the small,
beautifully pictured rooms and chapels of St Bridget of
Sweden and her daughter, St Catherine.

Meditation
*Yahweh himself sent me to prophesy against this Temple
and this city all the things you have heard. So now amend
your behaviour and actions, listen to the voice of Yahweh
your God, and Yahweh will relent about the disaster that
he has decreed for you.* (Jr 26:12-13)

St Catherine of Siena

Another saintly woman who worked tirelessly for the
return of the papacy from Avignon was Caterina Benincasa
(1347-1380). Caterina was Italian, the daughter of a dyer
from Siena. She too was a visionary, mystic, stigmatist,
and papal counsellor. By her prayer, impassioned letters
and preaching, she gathered a following that continually
lobbied for the return of the papacy. She succeeded, for in
1377, Pope Gregory XI, the last of the Avignon Popes,
brought the throne of Peter and the Curia, amongst scenes
of great rejoicing, back to Rome.

Sadly the joy was short lived. Gregory's death after
little more than a year, provoked a papal conclave of
animosity and sheer farce, which sadly precipitated the

Great Western Schism dividing the Church into two, and then three papal obediences from 1378, which was finally resolved in 1417 by the Council of Constance. Caterina, broken hearted by the Schism died in 1380 and was buried in St Mary sopra Minerva (see Our Lady in Rome, p. 64). The room where she died was turned into a votive chapel in the seventeenth century, and is accessible from the church. She was canonised as St Catherine of Siena in 1461, is a patron saint of Italy, and her life and writings are still widely followed and revered.

Meditation

You eternal Truth, have told me the truth: that love compelled you to create us. Even though you saw that we would offend you, your charity would not let you set your eyes on that sight. No, you took your eyes off the sin that was to be and fixed your gaze only on your creature's beauty. For, if you had concentrated on the sin, you would have forgotten the love you had for creating mankind. Not that the sin was hidden from you, but you concentrated on the love because you are nothing but a fire of love, crazy over what you have made. And I in my sinfulness have never known you! But give me the grace, dearest Love, that my body may give up its blood for the honour and glory of your name.

(From the Prayers of Catherine of Siena)

St Ignatius of Loyola

One of the powerful figures of the Counter Reformation was St Ignatius of Loyola (1491-1556), the founder of the Society of Jesus. He was a Spanish nobleman and soldier, born in the Basque region of Spain in 1491. It was on his lengthy recovery from battle wounds, where the only available readings were that of Christ and the saints, that he began his conversion from worldly courtier to that of pilgrim and missionary. After some turbulent times, over which his Ignatian Spiritual Exercises evolved, he came to Rome, already an ordained priest, and having formed with some other young men 'the Companions of Jesus'. In 1540 he received Papal approval for his society, from which this great Order grew, evangelising and preaching in the most hostile and unreceptive parts of the world, producing many martyrs of the Faith.

A visit to his rooms - adjacent to the beautiful Jesuit church, the Gesu - retained faithfully in the original, beautifully and thoughtfully presented, is well worth while. Here you can trace his history and that of the Society, and most movingly, pray in his private Chapel. After some peaceful reflective time in the chapel you can entertain yourself on your way out with the most amazing visual and perspective wizardry of the painted corridor outside his rooms, where shape and form of the whole corridor will slide from perfection to gross distortion and back again, depending on where you stand and look.

Prayer

Receive, Lord, all my liberty, my memory, my
understanding, and my whole will. You have given me
all that I have, all that I am, and I surrender all to your
divine will, in order that you may dispose of me. Give
me only your love and your grace. With this I am rich
enough, and I have no more to ask. (St Ignatius of Loyola)

St Philip Neri

Another prominent character of the Counter Reformation
was St Philip Neri (1515-1595), and although twenty five
years younger, was a friend and contemporary of St
Ignatius, of which was rather fittingly sealed with their
canonisation on the same day in 1622. St Philip was
known formally as the Apostle of Rome, more
informally, by those he ministered to, as Pippo Bono
(Good Phil). He evangelised thousands of people in
Rome, shamelessly button-holing individuals in life-
changing conversations. He worked tirelessly with the
poor young children of Rome, removing them from
squalor and degradation to places of safety, and giving
them instruction. He was also the friend and counsellor to
popes and cardinals, including St Charles Borromeo; a
indefatigable confessor, he had the gift of telling
penitents their sins before they confessed them.

He founded, in 1575, the Congregation of the Oratory,
a group of priests and laymen, dedicated to preaching and

teaching, an apostolate later taken on by Cardinal John Henry Newman in founding the English Oratory in Birmingham. He was well known for his informality and sense of humour - which actually hid a strict orthodoxy - summed up by one of his many bon mots: "If you want to be obeyed, don't make commandments". As the patron saint of humorists, he summed himself up with: "Cheerfulness strengthens the heart and makes us persevere in a good life. Therefore the servant of God ought always to be in good spirits."

The church of the Fathers of the Oratory of St Philip of Neri, formally titled St Mary in Valicella, but more frequently known as Chiesa Nuova (New Church), I found to be rather a careworn church, possibly brought on by first impressions in its not very attractive setting. Frustratingly, there was no access to St Philip's rooms attached for individual, casual visitors, my understanding is that they are only made available by prior arrangement for group visits.

Meditation
Cast yourself with confidence into the arms of God. And be very sure of this, if he wants anything of you he will fit you for your work and give you strength to do it.
(St Philip Neri)

≈ JOURNEY'S END ≈

CHURCH OF ST CLEMENT

Layers of Christianity

For me, my journey in Rome would end with a visit to the church of Saint Clement, a few minutes' walk from the Colosseum. And whilst this may not be entirely convenient in your own pilgrim programme, it is well worth calling in at some stage. Because here, in this one venue, is a lovely summary of the history of Christianity in Rome. For beneath the current twelfth century church lies the excavated remains and outline, complete with original altar, canopy and apse, of a fourth century, three-aisled church. And on the level beneath that, lies a private, first century house, a small fifth or sixth century catacomb with sixteen wall tombs, and just opposite where the house is, a pagan temple.

St Clement

It is not known with certainty who lived in the house at the bottom level: wishful deduction attributes ownership to St Clement, a holy priest from an Imperial Roman family, to whom the church above is dedicated, but there is no hard evidence for this.

However, soon after Constantine came to power in the fourth century, this and the surrounding area, was filled in with rubble to provide the bedrock on which the fourth century church, named after St Clement, was built. Clement, having known Ss Peter and Paul, went on from priesthood to becoming the fourth Pope in AD 88, suffering martyrdom in AD 97, under the Emperor Domitian's persecution. The church dedicated to him survived through to the Middle Ages as one of Rome's prominent Christian churches.

In 1084, it was razed to the ground by the Norman, Robert Guiscard, during the sack of Rome. The huge quantities of rubble from this wholesale destruction once again raised the level of the city. In 1108 construction of a new basilica began on top of the ruins of the old church. The remains of the old church disappeared from human sight for the next seven hundred and fifty years. The current church, came under the care of the Irish Dominicans in 1667, but it was not until 1857, as a result of the energetic explorations underground of one of the Irish priests, that what lay below started coming to light.

The fourth century church, along with precious eighth, ninth and tenth century paintings and mosaics, emerged from the excavations. Deeper digging led to the remains of the first century private house, and just across what was a narrow alleyway opposite, came to light a small temple dedicated to another competing religion of first century Rome - but long since gone - Mithraism. In this ancient *mithraeum* one looks on in some wonder at the small vaulted ceiling, stone benches, and small altar with clear bas-reliefs depicting the Persian deity Mithras sacrificing a bull to the sun.

Today's church

Today's church at street level, features typical aspects of a medieval church - mosaic adorned apse, a marble *baldachino* over the main altar, and a marble enclosed *schola cantorum*, or choir area. The early twelfth century mosaic in the apse, one of the most striking in Rome, is described as 'exuberant and flamboyant', charged with the symbolism of the Triumph of the Cross. The church also has, unusually for a city centre church, an atrium in the form of a spacious, open colonnaded area in front of the church, which in former days was the place where those receiving instruction before baptism, or those doing penance, remained whilst the sacred mysteries were being celebrated inside.

The presentation and visiting regime at St Clement's is quite low key - it is not crowded, there are no compulsory conducted tours underground. For a very modest sum you can linger, ponder and marvel over this two thousand year span at your leisure.

For me just this one site epitomised the trials and tribulations of our Catholic faith over the millennia -

against invasion, persecution, incursion by other
religions. It visibly reminds us of the resolution and
strength of the Faith - the constant and determined
building and rebuilding of the Kingdom on Earth over the
ruins of previous human folly, in the continuing attempt
to maintain and promote the Kingdom of Eternal Life. I
had discovered - at very least - what I had set out to do on
my Rome pilgrimage in this one set of buildings. I found
not only the roots, but the sturdy trunk and thriving
branches of our Faith, as well.

Meditation

*A metaphor of life, the pilgrimage becomes an
anticipation of the world that is to come, a pledge of the
Feast of the Kingdom, a renewed experience of the
encounter that changes the heart. This is because it
reveals God who illumines the things that have passed,
gives value to the present, and allows a foretaste of the
ultimate and future promises, and makes him loved. Let us
stay pilgrims in the night, but joyfully standing on the
word of the promise that came forth from Silence, anxious
before the question that can shake any easily found
certainty of faith. "When the Son of Man comes, will he
find any faith on earth? (Lk 18:8). Along this way we shall
be pilgrims clinging to the Word, echoing the word
'Maranatha', an invocation, a yearning, an expectation:
"Come Lord!".* (Official Vatican Guide for the Jubilee Year 2000)

∾ Suggested Itineraries ∾

Rome is a reasonably compact city in terms of getting to the places mentioned in this book. This Section may help in planning an itinerary: listed below are the venues mentioned in previous Sections (and some extras on the way!) grouped together in reasonable walking (or, if necessary, Metro/bus/tram) distance of each other. In all cases they are listed from West to East. In and amongst and around these you can also plan other places you may want to visit or come across on the way - but remember - it is not a marathon!

1. Vatican City: St Peter's and Square, Vatican shops and **Post Office**, **Vatican Museums** and **Sistine Chapel** (access through Museum complex), Vatican City **church of St Anna** (through the gate on Via Angelica Portica).

2. Beginning at Domine Quo Vadis? If you want to follow the Beginning Section, it is easily busable to St Sebastian's gate and then walking on to **Domine Quo Vadis?** (also easily busable). **The Catacombs of St Callistus** are a short walk from there, as is the **Catacombs and Basilica of St Sebastian** beyond that.

There is a profusion of places in the following two groups, and for convenience I split them respectively into North and South of the Corso Vittorio Emanuele II, although, of course, you can plan your own variations, depending on your particular interests.

3. North: Starting at **Chiesa Nuova (church of St Philip Neri)** - across to the splendid **Baroque Piazza Navona** for a refreshing coffee, watch the world go by, and admire Bernini's marvellous **Fountain of the Four Rivers**. Then across to the **Pantheon**, very close to which is **Santa Maria sopra Minerva**, and next door, the Jesuit **church of St Ignatius of Loyola**, with its cunning false dome. You may want to finish this leg by wandering up to the **Trevi Fountain** (usually very crowded - but there are two small churches just off the Plaza if you want some peace and quiet: **Santa Maria in Trivio** and **Ss Vincent and Anastasia**).

4. South: The **English College**, **St Bridget's church** (peaceful haven), and **rooms of St Bridget**, take a break in the lively piazza **Campo de Fiori**. A slightly longer walk across to the beautiful **Baroque of the Gesu** and the **rooms of St Ignatius**. Nearby the small **Adoration chapel Capella la Madonnella de St Marco**, directly off the pavement off **Piazza Venezia**, (take another break in around Piazza Venezia and **Victor Emmanuel Monument** (*Il Vittoriano*), and if you have the energy, a visit to the **Mamertine Prison**, close by.

5. Marian Churches: You could start this next group by visiting the slightly isolated **Santa Maria del Popolo** (Metro Flaminio), and then going on by tube to the

Capuchin church of **Santa Maria della Concezione**, with its vaulted chapels adorned with the skulls and bones of their departed brethren (Metro Barberini), across to **Santa Maria della Vittoria** - immediately opposite is **Santa Susanna (Mass in English)**. Take a break in the **Piazza della Republica** and its lively Fountain of the Naiads, and finally, head south to **St Mary Major**.

6. Trastevere is probably a bus or a taxi ride. If you feel like a bit of hill climbing, start with Bramante's tiny but perfectly formed circular 'temple', the **Tempieto di San Pietro in Montorio**, then downhill to **St Mary in Trastevere**. There are many lovely little pavement cafes in this old area of Rome. A visit to **St Cecilia in Trastevere** is worthwhile, and if time and energy permit, and you want some good pedestrian views of **Rome and the Tiber**, a walk across the **Ponte Sublicio** will take you to the 5th century **church of St Sabina**.

7. Colloseum Area: This last group takes in the **Colosseum**, the **church of St Clement**, **St John Lateran** and **Scala Santa**, ending with a walk through the park to the **Holy Cross in Jerusalem**.

8. Further Out: in the north east, **St Lawrence Outside the Walls** (bus or tram); in the south, **St Paul's Outside the Walls** (Metro St Paolo).

❦ ROME - A TIMELINE ❦

753 BC - The founding of Rome on the Palatine Hill, as told by the legend of Romulus and Remus, twins suckled by a she-wolf.

700 -506 BC - The Kingdom of Rome, period of the Etruscan Kings. Rome takes shape with the building of the Forum, the temple of Janus and the Cloaca Maxima, the first great sewer.

508 - 44 BC - The First Republic. Rome ruled by elected Consuls. Expansion of the Roman Empire to Italy, Spain, Greece, Syria. Ends with the assassination of Julius Caesar.

44 BC - Imperial Rome, a period of mainly despotic and cruel Emperors, under whom Rome continued to develop with such buildings as the Colosseum and the Pantheon.

42 AD - St Peter comes to Rome to an already existing Christian community.

67 AD - Martyrdom of Ss Peter and Paul under Nero. Population of Rome in Trajan's time (98) estimated at 1,000,000. Period of intermittent persecution of Christians.

313 AD - Freedom of worship for Christians granted by the first Christian Emperor,   Constantine, giving great impetus for the spread of Christianity round the Roman Empire. During this period Rome was invaded and sacked in turn by Visigoths, Huns and Vandals.

476 AD - Last of the Roman Emperors, Rome falls to Odoacer the Goth, who becomes King of Italy. Invasion and re-occupation of the city continues during this turbulent period. Rome, population down to 30,000, is at an all time low: "...buildings were crumbling into ruins; aqueducts and sewers were in urgent need of repair; monuments were dismembered..." (eyewitness account from Hibbert). Pope Gregory I (the Great) (590-604) makes great efforts to regain stability.

755 AD - Final split from Eastern Byzantium as Rome 'looks West' through Pope Stephen II's alliance with King Pepin of the Franks.

800 AD - Charlemagne, first Holy Roman Emperor (son of King Pepin), crowned in St Peter's on Christmas Day. There then follows an extended period, in Medieval times, of anarchy, greed and violence, from external invasion, warring local families, and scheming Popes. In the words of the Vatican, "Certainly, the history of the Popes is a tormented one and includes shadows. In some periods, intrigues and political factors cast dark clouds...".

1283 AD - Alliance with Charles of Anjou, King of Naples and Sicily, ensuring French influence over the papacy.

1300 AD - First Holy Year, declared by Boniface VIII.

1309-1377 AD - The Babylonian Captivity. Period when the papacy, under the influence of the French monarchy, moves to Avignon in France. Rome sinks further into decline and anarchy.

1378-1417 AD - The Great Western Schism where political and national ambitions split the papacy, at one period with three popes claiming to rule. The Church was reunited when Pope Martin V came to power.

mid 15th century - The Renaissance, a period of great contradiction with beautiful buildings and works of art transforming the city's appearance, but driven by some corrupt and materialistic popes.

early 16th century - The Reformation, the Protestant movement to reform the Church, in which Rome suffered grievously.

1527 AD - The Sack of Rome by German Emperor, Charles V. The city in ruins. An eye witness lamented, "Rome is finished, four fifths of it is quite uninhabitable".

mid 16th century - The Counter Reformation period of stringent reform in response to the Protestant Schism. Rebuilding of the city starts.

17th century - The Age of Baroque, generally an age of stability and calm, after the ravages of Reformation. The buildings and infrastructure of Rome are greatly enhanced with a new wave of architects and artists, "The gracious domes and cupolas, crowned by the mighty dome of St Peter's, were now prominent against the once medieval towers and fortresses. Fine palaces, elegant villas and sweeping gardens softened the once antagonistic and stark architecture that reflected the violence of ages past. And the travertine stone, favoured by the architects of Baroque, was now beginning to soften the cold marble of Renaissance". Population estimated at 150,000.

18th century - Development of Rome continues as a city, Catholicism flourishes; the 1709 census counted 240 monasteries, 73 convents, 23 seminaries and nearly 400 churches. The political influence of the papacy, however, wanes.

1798- 1815 AD - Rome occupied by the French and proclaimed a Republic; Pope Pius VII goes into exile, returning after the French ambitions in Europe collapse. Church's position threatened by secularism of the French Revolution.

19th century - Unification and monarchy, despite attempts by the papacy to resist unification, Rome is declared the capital city of a unified Italy and in 1870 occupied by royalist army of Victor Emmanuel, the first modern King of Italy. Huge expansion brings on a building boom, lamented by Augustus Hare, "Twelve years of Sardinian rule have done more for the destruction of Rome, with its beauty and interest, than the invasions of the Goths and Vandals".

1869 - 1870 AD - First Vatican Council convened by Pope Pius IX. Disrupted by Franco Prussian war, and adjourned; never formally closed. Dogma of Papal infallibility declared.

20th century - Fascism and War. The First World War has little impact on Rome. The post-war rise of fascism brings Mussolini to power.

1922 AD - Mussolini becomes Italy's Prime Minister; he had great designs on transforming Rome, "to appear wonderful to the whole world, immense, orderly and powerful, as she was in the days of the first empire of Augustus", destroying all that was "filthy and picturesque that smelled of the Middle Ages".

1929 AD - The Lateran Treaty, where Church and state formally separate. The Vatican accepts the State of Italy, with Rome as its capital, in exchange for sovereign independence for the Vatican, with the Pope as head of state.

1939 AD - Second World War. Rome occupied in September 1943 by Allied 1945 forces.

1946 AD - Italy a Republic, King Umberto II exiled.

1962 AD - Second Vatican Council convened by Pope John XXIII, and, **1965** closed by Pope Paul VI.

1978 - 2005 AD - Papacy of John Paul II.

2005 AD - Benedict XVI elected Pope, April 2005.

❧ INDEX ❧

Abbreviated Bibliography

HIBBERT, Christopher. *Rome - the Biography of a City*. London, Penguin Books, 1987.

MARCELIN-RICE, Kate (translated by). *St Peter's, Guide to the Square and Basilica*. Vatican City, Libreria Editrice Vaticana, 2004.

SIENKIEWICZ, Henryk. *Quo Vadis*. New York, Hippocrene Books, Inc, 2004.

WILD, Fiona (Proj ed). *Eye Witness Travel Guides* - Rome. London, Dorling Kindersley Ltd, 2004.

Informative Catholic Reading

We hope that you have enjoyed reading this booklet.

If you would like to find out more about CTS booklets - we'll send you our free information pack and catalogue.

Please send us your details:

Name ....

Address ....

....

....

Postcode ....

Telephone..

Email ....

Send to: CTS, 40-46 Harleyford Road,
            Vauxhall, London
            SE11 5AY

Tel: 020 7640 0042
Fax: 020 7640 0046
Email: info@cts-online.org.uk

 **CTS**